Heather
Buckingham
Given by Nanny in 1998

The Ultimate
FUN
CRAFTS
FOR KIDS

ISBN 1-898018-76-6

Design: Anita Ruddell
Photography: Jon Bouchier
Cover photography: James Duncan
Colour separation by P&W Graphics
Printed in Singapore by Toppan Ltd

The publisher would like to thank the staff and children of
Riversdale Primary School, London Borough of Wandsworth,
The Early Learning Centre, Phoebe Wood-Wheelhouse, Allie
Johnstone and Lewis Elwin for their help in producing the
photographs for this book.

The Ultimate
FUN
CRAFTS
FOR KIDS

Clare Beaton
Cheryl Brown
Jann Haworth
Miriam Haworth
Joan Jones
Irene Newington
Anita Ruddell

INDEX

Contents

Beads, Badges & Bangles

Masks

Paint

Presents

Fancy Dressing

Printing & Stencilling

What you will need

Before beginning the projects in this chapter, it is a good idea to collect together some tools first. You will need a roller to roll out paint and a flat surface to roll it on to (see page 8). Card and string come in useful for making blocks to print with and you will need a stencil brush and sponge for stencilling. Other useful tools are pictured here.

flat inking surface

round-ended knife

roller

Paint

Water-based paints and printing inks are used for almost all the projects in this book. You can use whichever you prefer. Buy the paint ready-mixed in large, easy-to-use, squeezy bottles. The printing inks come in tubes. The basic colours you will need are red, yellow, blue, black and white. From these you can mix all other colours. The paints and inks can be thinned by adding water to them.

Oil paints, fabric paints, fabric dyes and food colouring are also used and more information is given about these on page 256.

scissors

masking tape

paint-brushes

paints

spoon

Other Useful Things

Almost anything with a raised surface can be used for printing with, so do keep a look out for useful things around the home.
Here are some ideas:
corrugated card, bubble pack, corks, cotton reels, cardboard tubes, cut fruit and vegetables, leaves, buttons, off-cuts of wood, cloth, old shoes, keys, bottle tops, spent matches, shaped biscuit cutters.

tracing paper

metal
ruler

string

pencil and eraser

paper

craft
knife

oil pastels or
wax crayons

felt-tip
pens

ruler

printing
inks

glue

tissue
paper

sponge

stencil
brush

thick and
thin card

Remember

☆ Wear an apron and cover the work area.
☆ Collect together the items in the materials box at the beginning of each project.
☆ Always ask an adult for help when you see this sign ⚠
☆ Clear up after yourself.

7

Keep on Rolling

For many of the projects in this book you will need to roll out the printing ink or paint before you begin work. For this you will need a roller and a smooth flat surface such as an off-cut of plastic laminate, or you could use the shiny side of a piece of hardboard or a piece of thick polythene sheeting.

Rolling Out

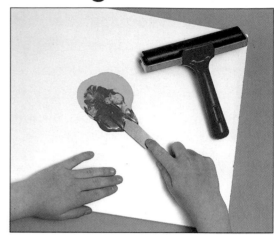

1 Put the paint on to the flat surface. Use a small round-ended knife to mix colours together.

2 Use a roller to roll out the mixed paint in all directions until there is an even layer of paint all over the surface.

3 You can now use the roller to transfer the paint on to a printing block ready to print.

Here are 2 ways to make a print directly from rolled out paint or ink. Roll out very thinly and work quickly as the ink dries very fast.

Transfer Print

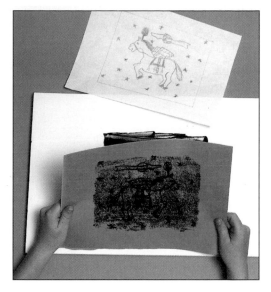

1 When the rolled out ink is nearly dry, lay a piece of coloured paper on to it and put one of your drawings on top. Firmly go over the drawing with a coloured pencil.

2 When you peel the coloured sheet off the inked surface you will see that you have made a print of your drawing.

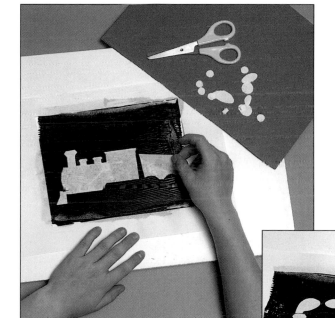

Paper Resist

1 Fold a piece of paper in half and cut a square from the folded edge. Open out and lay on to the rolled out ink. Cut out paper shapes and lay them on to the inked surface to make a picture.

Lightly dampen a sheet of paper and lay on top of the paper shapes.

2 Run a clean roller all over the back of the paper, and carefully lift off to reveal the print.

Letters and Numbers

With just 4 shapes cut from a potato you can print the whole alphabet and any number too.

1 Trace the 4 shapes on page 244 on to card and cut out.

⚠ 2 Cut a large potato into slabs about 1 cm thick. Draw around the card shapes on to the potato slabs and cut out.

3 Use a round-ended knife to mix and spread an even area of paint on to a flat surface.

4 Dip the potato shapes into the paint and try printing some letters.

MAKE A NAME PLAQUE

You can use the shapes to print out your name on to a piece of card. Why not print a border too. When the plaque is finished punch 2 holes at the top and thread through some ribbon so that you can hang it up on your bedroom door.

To print a border around the plaque, cut the end of a carrot into a heart shape. ⚠

5 Now try to print some numbers with your potato shapes.

This alphabet sampler shows you how to make all the letters of the alphabet with your potato shapes.

Bricks and Paper

This is the house that you built. . . from a small cardboard box!

Bricks and Tiles

⚠ **1** Ask an adult to cut a peeled potato into a 2-cm thick slab measuring about 3.5 cm x 7 cm. Cut thin grooves into the potato to look like bricks.

2 Dip the potato into red-brown paint and use it to print lines on to white paper.

⚠ **3** To make roof tiles, cut square-shaped grooves into a potato slab and use to print dark brown paint on to black paper.

Wallpaper

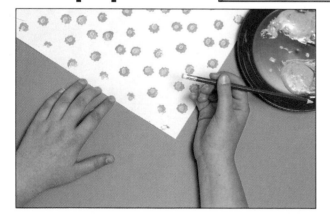

⚠ **4** Ask an adult to cut a flower shape from the end of a carrot and use it to print all over a large sheet of paper. Add some colour to the centre of the flower heads with a pencil-top eraser.

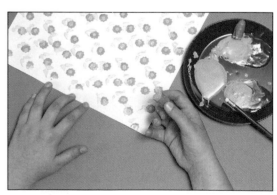

⚠ **5** Make a leaf stamp and use to print leaves at the base of the flower heads.

The House

6 To make a support to hold a roof cut 2 card triangles and tape to the front and back of the top of the house.

NOTE: The base of each triangle should be as wide as the side of the box.

7 Cut a rectangle of card to fit snugly between the 2 triangular supports and tape in place. Cover the box with the brick paper.

8 Cover a large piece of corrugated card with roof tile paper. Fold in half and tape to the roof supports.

To finish off the house paint the inside walls or cover them with the printed wallpaper. Make a 2-storey house by taping a piece of card in the middle of the box.

Wax Wonder

Make a beautiful rainbow-coloured print of one of your favourite drawings

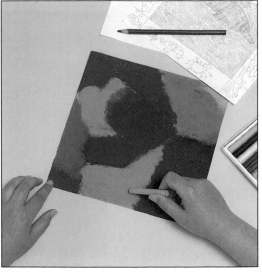

1 Cover a sheet of paper all over with oil pastels or wax crayons. Use bright colours, but avoid yellow as it does not transfer very well.

2 Put a clean sheet of paper on to the crayoned sheet, then put your drawing on top.

Make sure the edges of all 3 sheets of paper are lined up and keep together with paper clips.

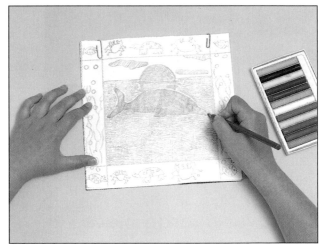

3 Go over your drawing with a coloured pencil, pressing firmly. This will transfer your drawing in colour on to the middle sheet of paper.

You can make as many prints as you like from your drawing, but do re-wax the crayoned sheet each time.

Mirror Image

A simple way to make a print of your face.

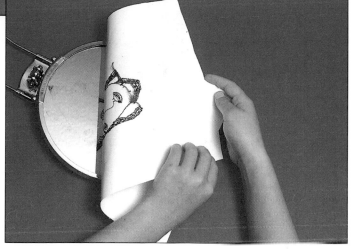

2 Lightly sponge a piece of paper to dampen it. Place the damp side on to the mirror and smooth flat all over.

1 Sit in front of a mirror. Close one eye. Use a washable fibre-tip pen to draw around your mirror image.

3 Lift off the paper to reveal your self-portrait.

This is the perfect way to draw a picture of yourself, but do make sure that you use a washable fibre-tip pen.

15

Fish in a Net

Make a simple printing block from corrugated card to print the fish and a roller from a cardboard tube and a piece of string to print the net.

1 Trace the large fish template on page 243 on to corrugated card and cut out.

2 Roll paint across the fish and use it to print on to coloured paper.

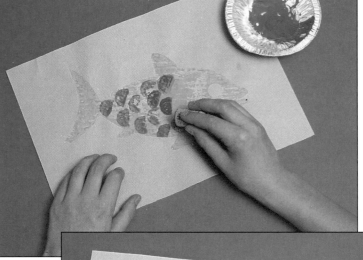

! **3** To make a stamp to print the scales on to the fish, ask an adult to cut away half of the end of a cork to make a semi-circle.

4 Use the rim of a bottle top to print the eye. Use a pencil-top eraser

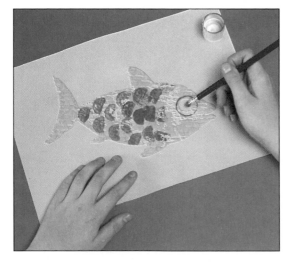

dipped into paint to print the centre of the eye.

5 Print the small fish with a shaped biscuit cutter. Alternatively, trace the template on page 243 on to card, cut out and use it to print with.

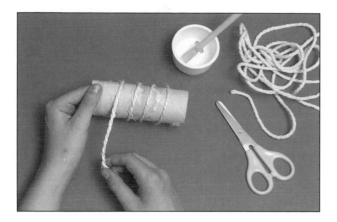

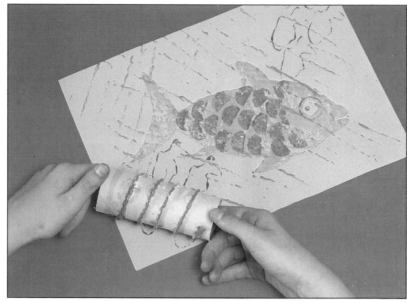

6 Glue string in a spiral around a cardboard tube.

Glue the finished picture in the centre of a large piece of coloured card. You could decorate the card frame with stencilled starfish and shells.

7 Roll the tube in paint until the string is completely covered. Roll diagonally over your picture both ways.

Surprise Tree

A cat and a bird are hidden amongst the branches of this tree printing block. There are templates for the cat and bird on page 243, but have a go at making the tree yourself.

1 Trace the cat and bird templates on page 243 on to thin card. Now draw a tree trunk and leaf shapes on to the thin card. Cut out all the shapes.

2 To make a frame glue 1-cm wide strips of card around the edges of a thick piece of card measuring 21 x 29.5 cm. Glue on the cut card shapes to make a tree picture. Leave to dry.

3 First make a rubbing of the finished picture. Put a piece of paper on top of the card and rub a wax crayon across the surface.

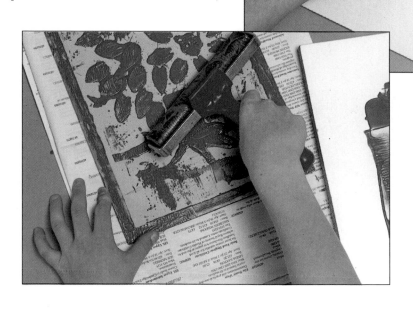

4 Now make a print. Roll paint all over the surface of the printing block.

18

5 Lay a piece of paper the same size as the printing block on top of it and carefully line up the edges. Rub firmly all over with the back of a spoon.

⚠ **6** Cut the end off a carrot to make a small circle. Dip in red paint and use it to print cherries all over the tree.

For a really special effect why not print over the cat and bird shape once again, but this time dip the cat and bird printing blocks in gold poster paint first.

7 Cut another cat and bird shape from thin card and glue on to the end of 2 corks. Dip into paint and use to print over the cat and bird shape in the branches of the tree.

19

Printing Press

You can make a printing block from polystyrene food packaging. Wash it well first.

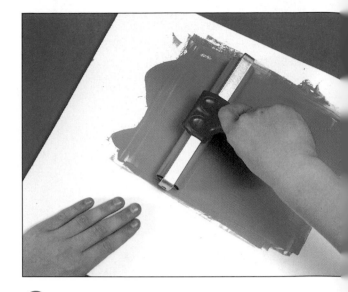

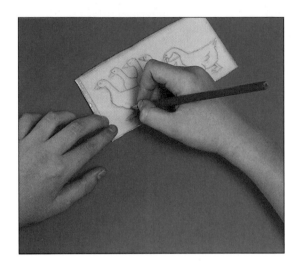

1 Make a tracing of a favourite picture. Tape the tracing to a piece of polystyrene cut to size. To transfer the drawing to the polystyrene, firmly go over it with a blunt, coloured pencil.

2 Roll out the printing ink on to a flat surface (see page 8). For a colour blend try rolling out 2 colours side by side, mixing a bit in the centre, then rolling backwards and forwards only.

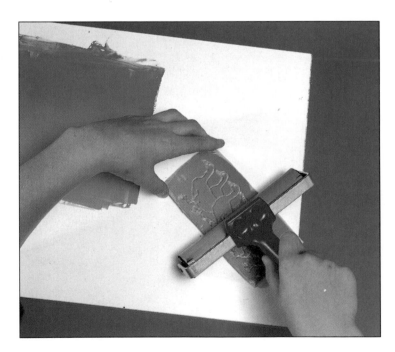

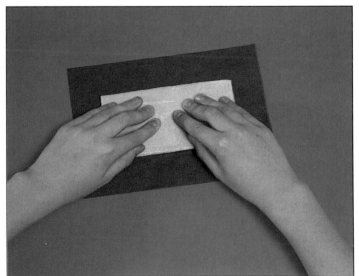

3 Roll the printing ink across the polystyrene printing block once.

4 Centre the polystyrene printing block on to a piece of paper and press down firmly.

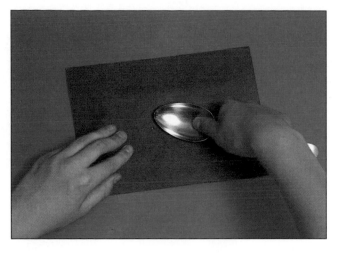

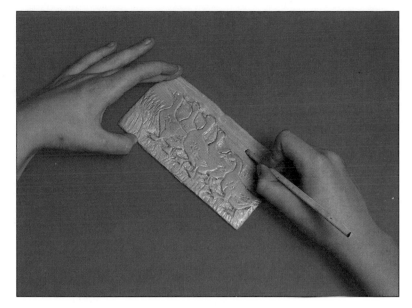

5 The paper will stick to the ink. Turn it over and rub firmly all over the paper with the back of a spoon to get an even print. Carefully lift off the polystyrene. Wash the polystyrene, roller and inking surface.

6 To add another colour to the picture, use a stick to press into the bits of the printing block that you do not want to print again.

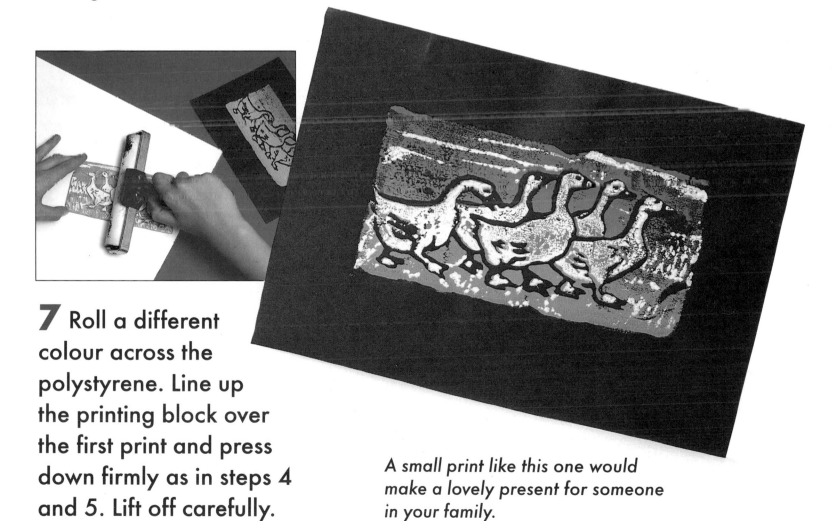

7 Roll a different colour across the polystyrene. Line up the printing block over the first print and press down firmly as in steps 4 and 5. Lift off carefully.

A small print like this one would make a lovely present for someone in your family.

Circus Wagons

Print a circus wagon frieze for your bedroom wall.

1 Fold an A4 sheet of paper in half and cut a rectangle from the folded edge. Open and place on another piece of A4 paper lining up the edges. Sponge paint all over the inside of the cut rectangle and leave to dry.

2 Trace the lion template on page 244 on to thick paper and cut out to make a stencil. Place the lion stencil in the centre of the sponged rectangle.

3 Dip a stencil brush into paint. Dab the brush up and down all over the inside of the stencil taking care that the paint does not seep under the edges.

4 Print the edges of the wagon using strips cut from corrugated cardboard.

5 Use a cut cork and carrot to print the top of the wagon. Print on the wheels with the cut carrot. Use a pencil-top eraser to add the finishing touches.

6 Cut a stencil for the lion's mane (template page 244). Carefully line up on the lion's head and stencil with dark brown paint.

7 Use the edge of a piece of thick card to print the cage bars.

Use the leopard and giraffe templates on page 244 to make more circus wagons. Glue the printed wagons on to thin card and cut out. Join together the 3 wagons with bits of string and stick to a piece of black card.

Balancing Butterfly

Amaze your friends by effortlessly balancing this butterfly on the end of a pencil.

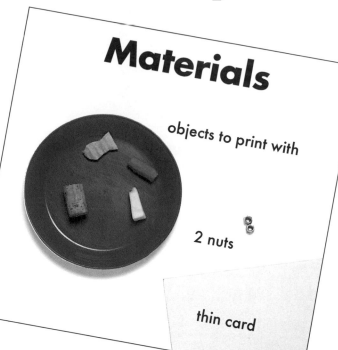

Materials

objects to print with

2 nuts

thin card

1 To make a stencil trace the butterfly on page 243 on to paper and cut out.

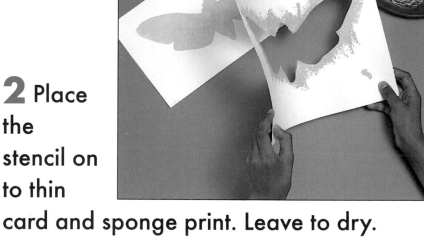

2 Place the stencil on to thin card and sponge print. Leave to dry.

3 Decorate the butterfly by printing all over it with cut vegetables, cut card, erasers or any other objects dipped into paint.

4 When the butterfly is dry, cut it out.

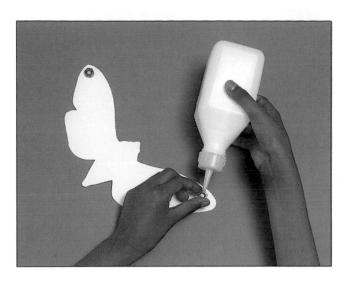

5 Glue the nuts to the top corners of the back of the wings.

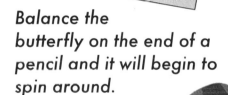

BLOT BUTTERFLIES
Draw half a butterfly along the folded edge of a piece of paper. Cut out and open flat. Drop blobs of paint on to one half of the butterfly, fold over and press firmly. Open and leave to dry.

What a colourful display. The blot butterflies on the right are very easy to make.

Balance the butterfly on the end of a pencil and it will begin to spin around.

25

Dino Print

Bring new life to an old T-shirt with this fantastic dinosaur stencil. All you need are fabric paints.

1 Trace the dinosaur and footprint templates on page 244 on to thin card and cut out to make the stencils.

2 Put a piece of card, covered with blotting paper, inside a washed and ironed T-shirt.

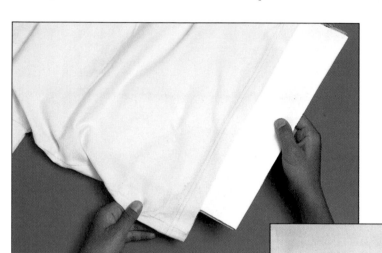

3 Tape the stencil in the centre of the T-shirt. Mask off the rest of the T-shirt by taping paper all around the stencil. Dip a stiff brush into the fabric paint. Test on paper first, and then with a dabbing up and down motion paint all over the stencil.

4 Remove the paper and carefully lift off the stencil. Leave to dry.

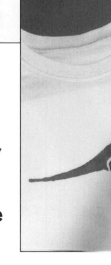

5 Use tailor's chalk to mark on the trail of footprints.

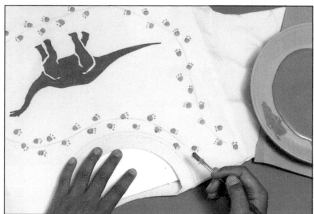

7 Use a small brush to add the 3 toe markings to finish off each footprint.

6 Stencil the footprints along the marked trail. Protect the T-shirt from paint splashes by laying a large piece of paper that has had a rectangle cut from the middle of it over the footprint stencil.

The finished T-shirt.

⚠ 8 To fix the fabric paint, cover the stencilled area with a clean cloth, and press with a hot iron for 2 minutes.

27

Japanese Paper Fold

All you need to make this printed paper is paper, food colouring and a rubber band. But it is worth remembering that the thinner the paper you use, the easier it will be to fold.

1 Fold over the edge of the paper by 2 cm and press down. Turn over  and fold over by 2 cm again. Repeat until all the paper has been folded.

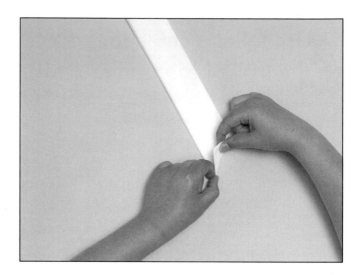

2 Holding the paper fan together, fold the bottom right corner to the left edge to make a triangle.

3 Turn over and fold the triangle straight up, pressing firmly with your fingertips.

4 Turn over and fold the bottom left corner to the right edge to make a triangle.

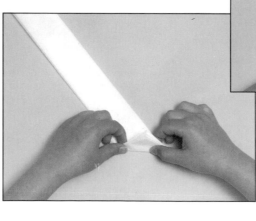

5 Turn over and fold the triangle straight up, pressing firmly once again.

28

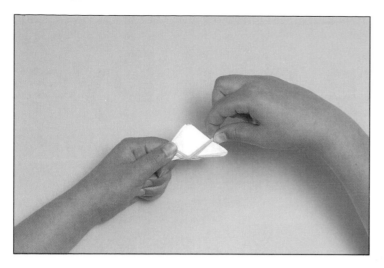

6 Continue folding as in steps 2 to 5 until you reach the top of the paper. Finish with a triangle fold. To hold the folded paper triangle together, put the rubber band around one corner, twist it and loop over the opposite corner.

7 Put undiluted food colouring into three small dishes. Dip each edge of the folded paper triangle into a different colour, leaving the centre white.

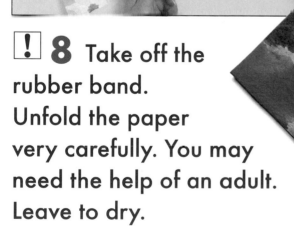

!8 Take off the rubber band. Unfold the paper very carefully. You may need the help of an adult. Leave to dry.

The finished paper makes beautiful gift wrapping. Or try taping a tissue-paper sheet to a window for a stained glass effect.

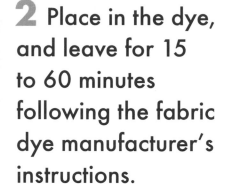

Tie and Dye

Have fun with this traditional way of printing patterns on to fabric.

Circles

1 Pick up a fabric square in the centre and tie firmly in 3 places with string that has been waxed with a candle.

Marble

Scrunch up a fabric square and tie with waxed string, criss crossing the string over itself many times. Follow steps 2-4.

Tile Squares

Fold the fabric square up into a small square. Sandwich the folded fabric between 2 blocks of wood and tie tightly. Follow steps 2-4.

2 Place in the dye, and leave for 15 to 60 minutes following the fabric dye manufacturer's instructions.

How you tie the fabric before dying can produce very different results.

Beans

Lightly pencil a pattern of dots on to a fabric square. Centre a bean on each pencil dot and tie in place with waxed string. Follow steps 2-4.

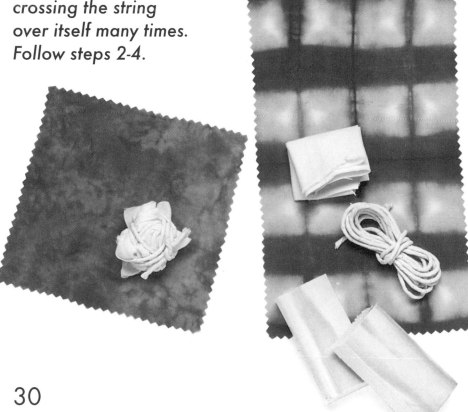

3 Use a pair of tongs or a fork to lift out the fabric from the dye,

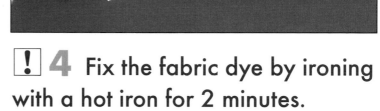

and rinse under cold water. Untie the string. Open out the fabric and leave to dry.

Broad Stripe

Fold over the edge of the fabric square by 2 cm. Turn over and fold over by 2 cm again. Repeat until all the fabric has been folded into a fan. Tie broad stripes of waxed string at intervals along the folded fabric. Dye and rinse. Undo some of the string to the original colour. Tie more string around the freshly dyed areas and then dip into a second colour dye. Follow steps 3-4.

! **4** Fix the fabric dye by ironing with a hot iron for 2 minutes.

Seven Colours

Follow the instructions for Broad Stripe. Now fold the dyed fabric square into a fan the opposite way. Tie with broad stripes of waxed string along the folded fabric and dip into a third colour dye. Follow steps 3-4.

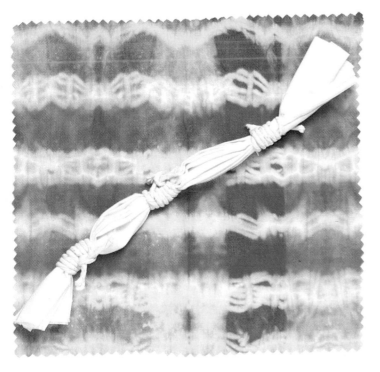

Materials

white spirit

2 pots of oil paint

strips of newspaper

plastic tray

Plastic fork

1 litre of gelatine !

printing paper

Marbling

To get the best results, you do need to use oil paints for marbling. These will stain, so do be careful.

! **1** Squeeze 2 different colours of oil paint into separate containers. Mix white spirit into the oil paints to make them slightly runny.

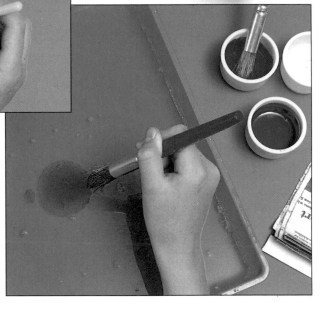

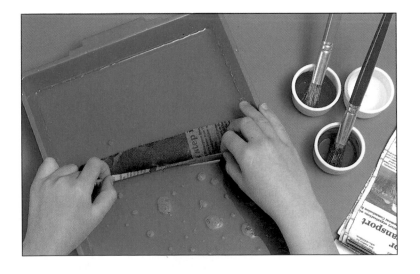

2 Pour the gelatine into the shallow tray and skim the surface with a strip of newspaper.

3 Shake a drop of the paint on to the skimmed surface. If the drop spreads into a circle larger than a milk bottle top it is too thin – add more paint. If the paint drops to the bottom of the tray, it is too thick – add a drop more white spirit.

32

5 Holding a piece of paper at opposite ends, lower it on to the surface of the gelatine and smooth to get rid of any air bubbles. Lift off and leave to dry. To make another piece of marbled paper, skim the surface with the newspaper strip and repeat from step 4.

Try dropping one colour inside the centre of another and watch it spread the first colour. Or use a comb to spread the paint across the skimmed surface.

4 When the consistency of the paint is just right, skim the surface with the newspaper strip again. Drop the 2 different colours on to the surface of the gelatine, and use a plastic fork to gently move the paint around to form patterns.

To make your own card stationery: dip only the edges of a piece of card into the tray.

Marbled paper can be used to cover tins, books, scrap books or for wrapping paper. To flatten the marbled paper leave it under a heavy book overnight.

33

Collage

What you will need

In this chapter you will find out how to make pictures and objects by sticking all sorts of bits and pieces on to a background. That background might be paper, a box, a bottle or even an old plastic container. Before you begin the projects in this chapter it is a good idea to collect together some useful things. A variety of different papers and glue are your basic tools (see page 36) but all sorts of other things will come in useful too.

double-sided tape

pinking shears

pair of compasses

clear tape

scissors

masking tape

paint-brushes

toothbrush

brown paper tape

paint

Other Useful Things

All sorts of things come in useful for making collages. Start a collection and keep adding to it. Store useful odds and ends in a box. Your collection might include:

Cardboard tubes, plastic containers, glass bottles and jars, bottle tops, jar lids, old newspapers and magazines, corrugated cardboard, coloured card and coloured paper, gold and silver foil, gummed paper, crêpe paper, tissue-paper, wool, string, gold and silver thread, cellophane and sweet wrappers, glitter, confetti, stickers, buttons, sequins, felt, material off-cuts, ribbons, metal scraps, nuts and bolts.

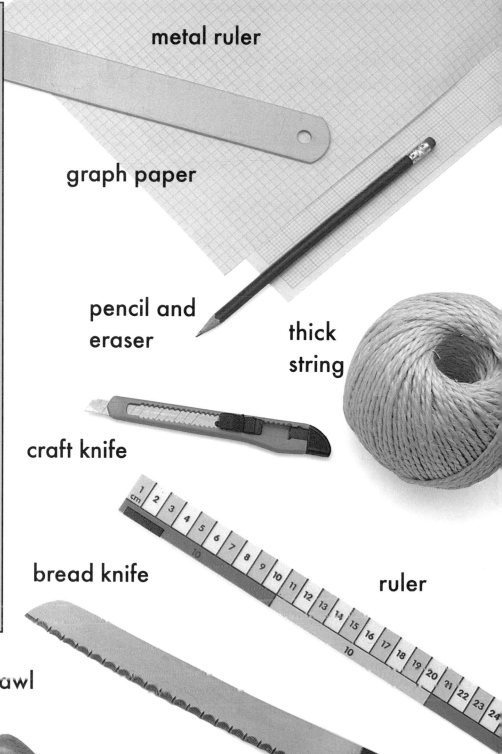

metal ruler

graph paper

pencil and eraser

thick string

craft knife

bread knife

ruler

bradawl

wire cutters

hammer

Remember

☆ Wear an apron and cover the work area.
☆ Collect together the items in the materials box at the beginning of each project.
☆ Always ask an adult for help when you see this sign !
☆ Clear up after yourself.

35

Paper and Glue

You can make exciting collages using just paper and glue. It's a good idea to set aside a box to store different kinds of paper in. Keep a look out for different colours and textures. Save old magazines, wrapping papers, the labels off tins, used stamps, paper bags, newspapers, used envelopes, junk mail, and interesting cardboard boxes.

Wallpaper paste for papier mâché and making paper. You can paint and draw over this but it takes 24 hours to dry.

PVA is strong and quick drying. You can also use it to brush over your finished work to make it look shiny.

Glue stick won't wrinkle paper.

Tear and Cut

You can make an interesting collage by mixing shapes that you have carefully cut out together with shapes that you have torn from paper.

Tissue-paper Weave

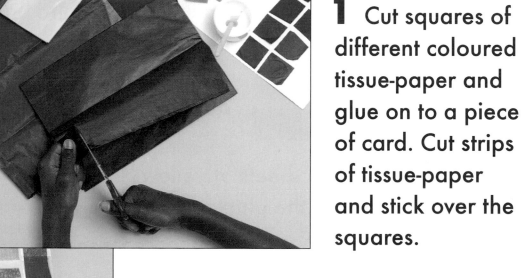

1 Cut squares of different coloured tissue-paper and glue on to a piece of card. Cut strips of tissue-paper and stick over the squares.

2 Paste a few more tissue-paper squares on top of the strips. Paste PVA glue all over the finished picture to make it look shiny.

Nothing Wasted

Cut shapes from paper, such as circles, squares, rectangles, leaves and hearts. Make a picture by sticking the cut shapes and the paper they were cut from on to a piece of card.

Tiger! Tiger!

A simple collage of a bright, bouncing tiger made by gluing layers of tissue-paper on to card.

Materials

tissue-paper

large sheet of cardboard

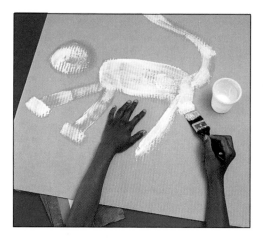

1 Use a large brushful of glue to paint the head and body of a tiger on to the cardboard sheet. Use more glue to paint on the legs and tail. You will need to work quickly before the glue dries.

2 Smooth 1 or 2 sheets of yellow tissue-paper over the glue-painted tiger. Leave to dry overnight.

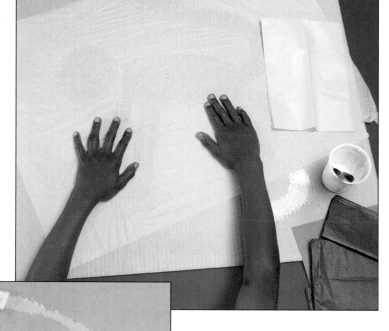

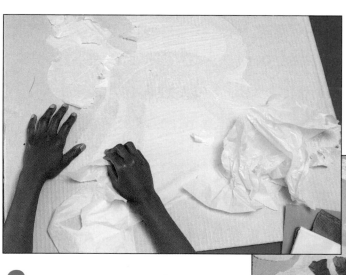

3 Tear away the unglued tissue-paper to leave the outline of the tiger.

4 Glue torn tissue-paper strips and shapes on to the tiger outline to add detail.

38

5 Now add some background detail, but keep it simple so that the tiger stands out – a yellow semi-circle for the sun, blue strips for the sky and green and yellow strips for the grass.

The finished picture. When you are adding detail to the tiger outline in step 4, it might help if you copy a picture of a tiger from a book.

When adding the black and white stripes, don't worry if they come off the edge of the tiger. This will give a feeling of movement.

To make the frame see page 40.

39

Frame Up

All you need to make this frame is one side of a cardboard box. If the picture to be framed is very large like this one, you'll need a very large cardboard box.

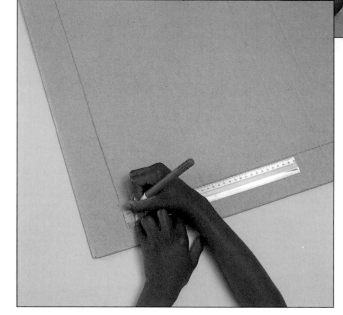

1 Cut a piece of cardboard exactly the same size as your picture.

⚠ **2** Rule a line along each side of the cardboard 6 cm from the edge. Ask an adult to cut out the marked off area in the middle to make a frame.

3 The piece of card cut from the centre of the frame is used to decorate it. Cut the card into strips, squares and triangles that will fit along the edge of the frame.

4 Use the cut cardboard shapes to make a pattern along the frame and glue them in place. Paint and leave to dry.

5 Brush glue all the way around the edge of the back of the frame. Put the picture front side down on to the glue, press around the edges firmly and leave to dry.

6 Make a hole in the top 2 corners of the frame. Thread about 1 metre of thick string through the holes and tie a knot at each end.

Ask your mum or dad to help you find a place to hang up your pictures so that everyone can admire them.

A. B. The Robot

Metal jar lids, broken chains and discarded keys will all come in useful to make this collage.

TIP BOX ⚠️
Use a hammer to flatten bottle and jar lids and old tin cans to use in your metal collage. The best place to do this is outside on cement.

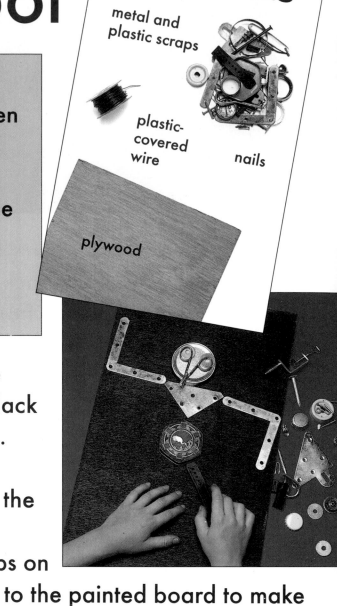

Materials
metal and plastic scraps

plastic-covered wire

nails

plywood

1 Paint the plyboard black on one side.

2 Arrange the metal and plastic scraps on to the painted board to make a picture of a robot.

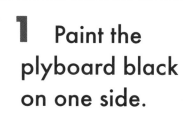

3 Once you have made a picture that you are happy with, glue the metal and plastic bits in place with strong glue.

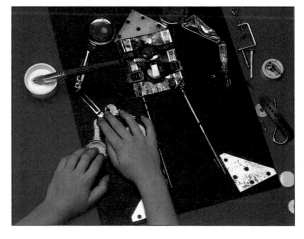

4 ⚠️ You can also use screws to secure the metal scraps, or hammer them in place with carpet tacks.

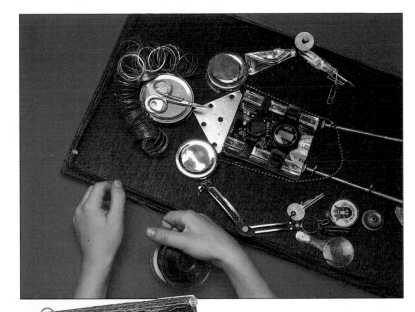

5 [!] To make a frame for your picture, hammer 2-3 nails along each side of the plyboard.

6 Wind plastic-covered wire several times around the nail frame.

Why not make up a story about your robot. This one's called Auntie Barbara and she babysits for tool boxes.

43

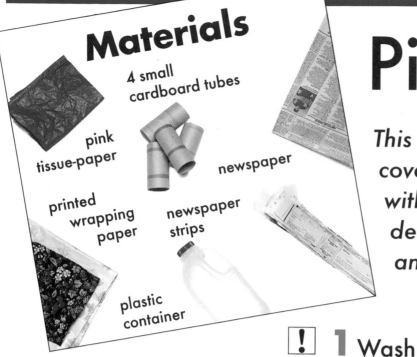

Materials

4 small cardboard tubes

pink tissue-paper

newspaper

printed wrapping paper

newspaper strips

plastic container

Pig Bank

This money box is made by covering a used plastic container with papier mâché, and then decorating it with tissue-paper and a collage of cut-out pictures.

[!] **1** Wash the plastic container well in warm soapy water and leave to dry. Ask an adult to cut off the handle.

2 To make the pig's legs cut tabs two-thirds the way around one end of the cardboard tubes. Bend back the tabs and tape a cardboard roll to each corner of the plastic container.

3 Brush the pig with wallpaper paste and lay on newspaper strips crossing them over each other as go. Continue in this way until the pig is completely covered (apart from its nose).

4 Cover the pig with at least 3 layers of papier mâché. Where the legs join the body add extra strips for a strong join.

44

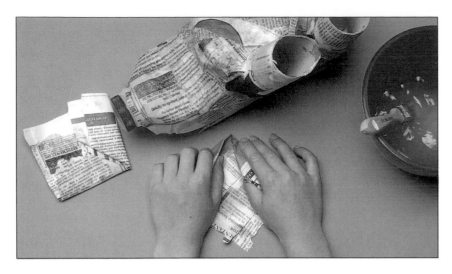 

5 To make each ear tear a few pieces of newspaper roughly the same size. Brush with paste and place on top of each other. Fold to a point at one corner.

6 To make a tail, twist together several strips of pasted newspaper.

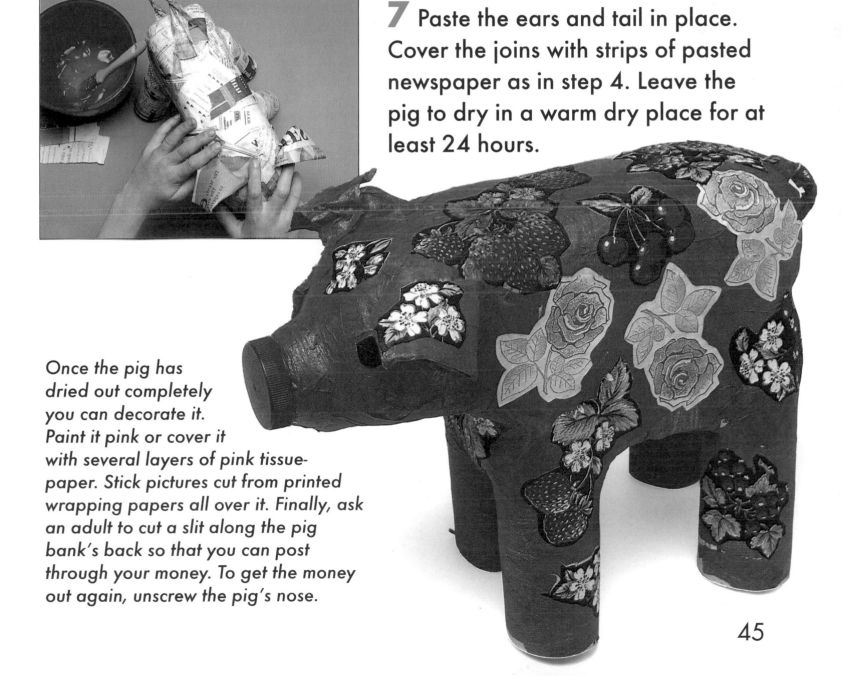

7 Paste the ears and tail in place. Cover the joins with strips of pasted newspaper as in step 4. Leave the pig to dry in a warm dry place for at least 24 hours.

Once the pig has dried out completely you can decorate it. Paint it pink or cover it with several layers of pink tissue-paper. Stick pictures cut from printed wrapping papers all over it. Finally, ask an adult to cut a slit along the pig bank's back so that you can post through your money. To get the money out again, unscrew the pig's nose.

45

Materials

glitter

air hardening modelling clay

picture scraps

salt

bottle or jar

Salt Bottles

This is a great way to recycle empty glass jars and bottles. Choose ones with a wide neck and wash them out well first in warm soapy water.

1 Brush glue all over the front of a cut out picture.

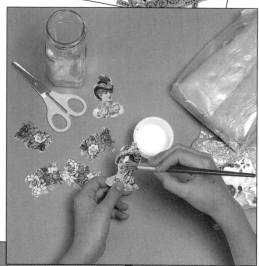

2 Slide a brush under the glued picture and lift it into an empty dry bottle. Press the picture against the glass and smooth down with the brush.

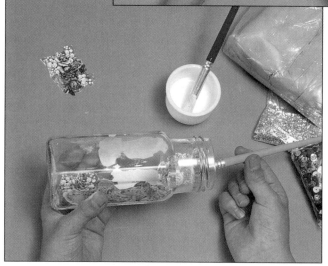

4 To make a stopper, roll a lump of air-hardening clay into a ball between your hands. The rolled ball should be big enough to fit into the neck of the bottle.

3 Now add more pictures, leaving some space between them. When you have finished decorating the bottle, leave it overnight to give the glue time to dry.

5 Roll in glitter and glue on sequins to decorate. Leave overnight to dry.

6 Next day, fill the decorated bottle with salt and glue the stopper in place.

To decorate the bottles you can either buy Victorian picture scraps or cut pictures from magazines or printed wrapping papers.

Do make a stopper for the salt-filled bottles. You could use a table tennis or tennis ball instead of air-hardening clay.

You could tie a ribbon around the neck of the decorated jar or bottle to finish it off.

Boo!

Transform a cardboard crate into this terrific mask.

Materials

- brown paper
- long stick
- coloured paper
- towelling rope
- cardboard crate box

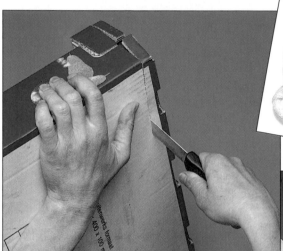

! **1** Ask an adult to cut the end off the box. A bread knife is probably best for this.

2 Mark a triangular point on to the cut end of the box.

! **3** Ask an adult to cut out the shape you have marked.

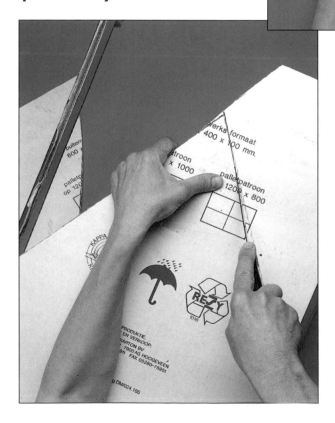

! **4** Ask an adult to score along the sides of the box at the base of the triangular shape.

48

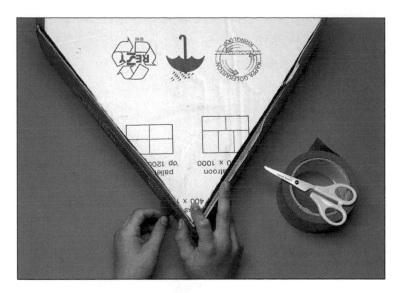

5 Bend the sides of the box in along the scored lines and tape them to the triangular shape with brown paper tape.

6 Cover the mask with brown paper. Cut shapes from coloured paper to make a face and glue in place.

Glue the towelling rope to the top of the mask to make hair. The finished mask, attached to a long stick, is big enough for two to hide behind.

Gift Boxes

Old boxes and containers decorated with cut-out paper shapes make lovely presents. So start collecting!

Materials

boxes

coloured paper

tissue-paper

1 Cover the box with plain paper. You can either use strips of paper or cut the paper exactly to fit.

2 Cut hearts and flower shapes from the tissue-paper.

3 Decorate the box with the cut out shapes glued in place.

4 To make the decorated box look shiny, brush all over with PVA glue. Leave to dry.

50

5 Cut leaves and flowers from the coloured paper. Stick the flowers on to the box. You can make the leaves stick up by putting glue on one end only.

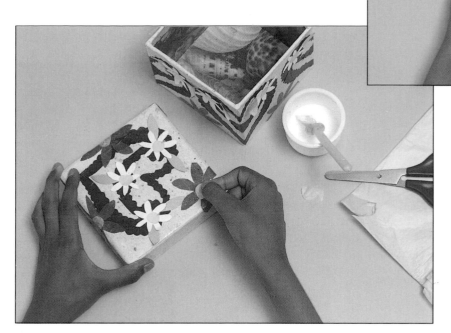

6 Glue a circle of yellow tissue-paper to the centre of each flower.

You can decorate a box with shapes that have been cut and torn from tissue-paper and glued in place.

Fill the decorated boxes with sweets or biscuits and give as a gift.

Pen Pals

Create your own matching stationery. Make sure the writing paper fits snugly into the envelope when it is folded in half or quarters.

1 Cut out some pictures from comics, magazines or printed wrapping papers.

2 Decorate the front of the envelope with the cut-out pictures and sticky stars. To re-use an old envelope, make sure that you cover the address and stamp.

With stationery that looks this good, everyone will want to get a letter from you.

3 Decorate the edges of the paper by sticking on cut-out pictures to match the envelope.

4 You can also glue on shapes torn from coloured paper, but do make sure that you leave enough space to write a message!

MAKING A SEAL
Pencil your initials *backwards* on to a small piece of card. Glue string along the pencil lines and leave to dry. To seal a used envelope mix flour and PVA glue into a paste and put a blob on to the flap. Press your initial stamp into the mixture and carefully lift off. Leave to dry before posting.

Mosaic

This picture is built up from squares of coloured paper.

1 Decide what you would like to be the subject of your mosaic. Draw your design on to graph paper and colour in the squares.

2 Cut strips of paper the same width from all the different colours that you are going to need to complete your picture.

3 Cut the strips into small squares. Keep the colours separate.

4 Take a large sheet of paper and, following your graph paper design carefully, paste the coloured squares on to the paper to make your mosaic picture.

54

5 Try to keep the squares in even rows and columns. You may have to trim some of the squares as you go to keep them in line with each other.

When choosing a design for your mosaic, you will find that a symmetrical design is best.

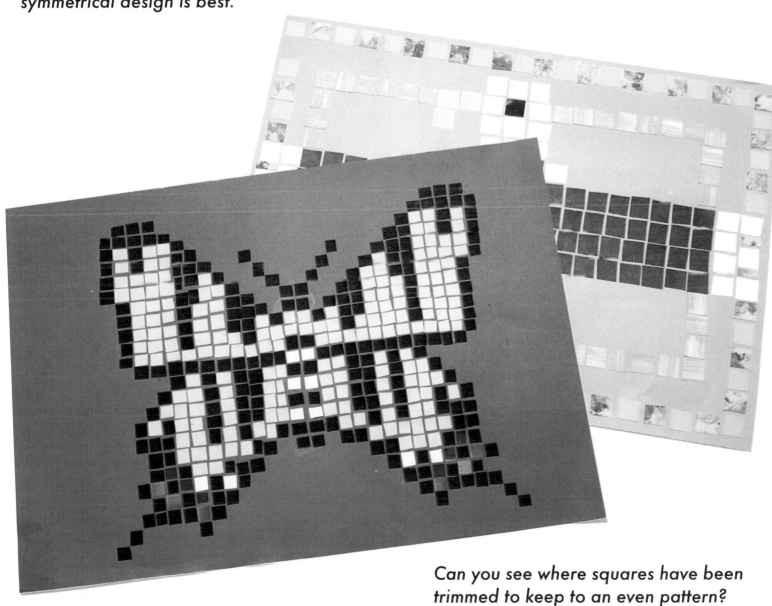

Can you see where squares have been trimmed to keep to an even pattern?

Dragon Kite

This tissue-paper kite will roar through the air on a breezy day.

Materials

coloured paper

2 garden sticks

string

tissue-paper

1 Make a cross from the 2 garden sticks and tie in the centre with string. Wind masking tape around the ends to make a raised edge.

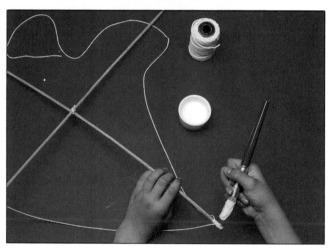

2 Fold a long bit of string in half and loop around one point of the cross. Glue in place.

3 Loop the string around the second and third points of the cross, and pull tightly. Tie the ends of the string together at the fourth point. Secure the string at each point with a blob of glue and leave to dry.

4 Glue tissue-paper over the front of the kite frame and decorate with eyes and a mouth cut from paper.

5 Cut slits along a piece of folded tissue-paper and tape

under the mouth. Make another 2 and tape to the top corners.

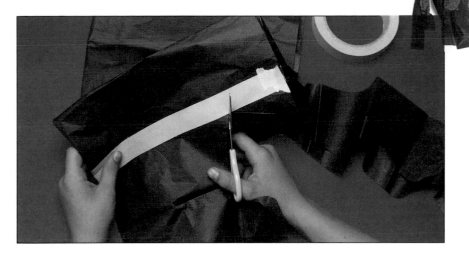

6 To make the dragon's tail, tape together 2 pieces of tissue-paper. Fold in half lengthways and cut a wavy line along one edge. Open out and use tape to attach to the kite frame.

7 On the back of the kite frame tie 3 pieces of string each measuring about 30 cm to the middle and top 2 points of the frame. Knot the ends of the guide strings together.

You can add some decoration to the dragon's tail to make it look even more stunning.

Tie a small ball of string to the guide strings and you are ready to fly your kite.

Paper Making

Materials shown (photo):

liquidizer · large deep bowl · bucket · dried flowers · kitchen cloth · selection of papers · net curtain · food colouring · newspaper · 2 wooden frames · drawing pins · glitter · tissue-paper

Paper making is fun to do, but it does take a little time to set up and you will need an adult's help.

! 1 Cut a piece of net about 10 cm larger all around than the frame. Fold over each edge and pin to the sides of the frame making sure that the net is stretched tightly.

2 Tear or cut the paper into thin strips and pieces and put in to the bucket. Cover with water and soak overnight.

! 3 Put a handful of soaked paper into the liquidizer adding more water when necessary. Liquidize for 15 seconds at a time until the pulp is creamy and well blended.

4 Put the blended pulp into a container that is larger than

the frame. Continue to liquidize the rest of the soaked paper until it has all been pulped. Add a little wallpaper paste to the pulped paper to help bind it together.

5 The pulped paper should not be as thick as porridge, but more like single or double cream. Add more water if necessary.

6 To make a couching bed to lay your homemade paper on to, place about 24 pages of newspaper on to a flat surface. Place a kitchen cloth on top of the newspaper.

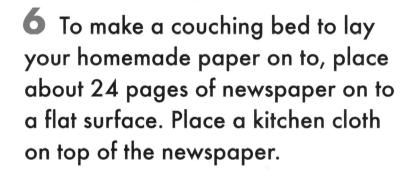

8 Slowly lower the frames into the pulp and carefully lift back out again. You should not be able to see the net through the pulped paper. Drain the frames over the bowl.

7 Take the net-covered frame, ***net side up***, and place the other frame on top of it.

Continues on next page

9 Take off the top frame and carefully place the net-covered frame, pulp side down, on to the couching bed. Press firmly with a cloth all over the net to wipe away any water.

If you want to make more than about 5 sheets of paper at a time you will need to make a second couching bed.

10 To loosen the paper from the net, gently rock the frame from side to side. If it sticks in places, give the back of the net more firm wipes.

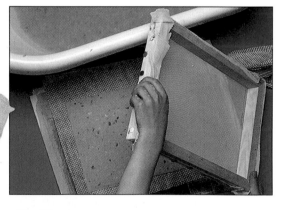

11 Lift off the frame.

To make homemade paper you need paper, so start collecting all you can including old envelopes, newspapers, paper napkins, kitchen roll and computer paper.

12 You can add decorative materials to the paper such as tissue-paper shapes, dried flowers and glitter.

13 And you can use drops of food colouring to stain it different colours.

The paper will take about 24 hours to dry but you can speed this up by laying each sheet of paper, still sandwiched between its kitchen cloths, on to dry newspaper in a warm place. If the paper begins to curl as it dries lay something heavy on top of it. Once the paper has dried, carefully peel away the kitchen cloth.

14 Before making a second sheet of paper, lay a kitchen cloth over the decorated paper, put several layers of newspaper on top, and finally another kitchen cloth. Continue from step 6.

Christmas Crafts

What you will need

In this chapter you'll find all sorts of imaginative ideas for Christmas. But before you begin any of the projects make sure you get together a few useful tools first. You'll need scissors or pinking shears for cutting (ask a grown up to cut thick card for you with a craft knife); a pair of compasses for making circles; a bradawl and a hole punch to make holes; glue, tape and staples to fix things together; and a needle and thread ready for sewing. Paint, felt-tip pens and fabric crayons will all come in useful for decorating.

needle and thread

clear glue

pliers

PVA glue and spreader

felt-tip pens

plastic tape

paint-brushes

clear tape

masking tape

paint

double-sided tape

glitter glue

Kitchen Equipment

To make the delicious Christmas biscuits and sweets on pages 68, 69 and 74-75 of this book, you will also need some standard kitchen tools including:

Pair of scales, measuring jug, measuring spoons, mixing bowls of various sizes, sieve, plastic spatula, cutlery, baking tray, greaseproof paper, chopping board, rolling pin, biscuit cutters, oven gloves.

Tubes of icing sugar, available in different colours from supermarkets and cake decorating shops, are a great way to decorate the biscuits.

tracing paper

craft knife

thick card

pencil and eraser

metal ruler

pinking shears

scissors

bradawl

stapler and staples

pair of compasses

hole punch

crayons

Remember

☆ Wear an apron and cover the work area.
☆ Collect together the items in the materials box at the beginning of each project.
☆ Always ask an adult for help when you see this sign [!]
☆ Clear up after yourself.

ruler

63

Christmas Tree

Begin the countdown to Christmas with this advent tree calendar.

Materials

24 wrapped sweets

24 15-cm lengths of ribbon

corrugated cardboard

sticky shapes

cocktail stick

tinsel

1 Mark 2 large triangles the same size on to corrugated cardboard. Mark a 5 mm slot from the centre to the top of one triangle and from the centre to the base of the other triangle. Cut out.

2 Paint the triangles green on both sides and leave to dry. Starting 5 cm from the base of one triangle, pierce 12 holes at regular intervals 1 cm from the edge along both sides.

3 Decorate both sides of both triangles with the sticky shapes. Slot the triangles together.

4 Securely tie a sweet to each piece of ribbon. Thread each ribbon through a hole and tie in a bow.

64

5 Glue tinsel to the other 2 edges of the tree.

Each day, from the first of December, take one sweet from the tree and eat it. When there are no more sweets left on the tree, it's Christmas Eve!

7 To make a star, trace off the template on page 245 on to card and paint yellow. When dry, paint all over with gold glitter paint. Attach to the tree with a cocktail stick.

Crackers for Christmas

To make your own Christmas crackers, all you need are a few readily-available materials and some good Christmas jokes. So get cracking!

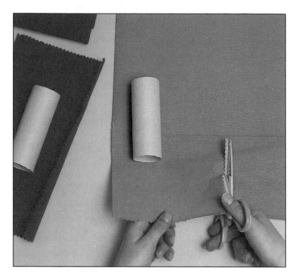

1 Use pinking shears to cut a piece of red crêpe paper twice as long as a cardboard tube. It should be wide enough to go around the tube with a 1 cm overlap. Cut a piece the same size from the green crêpe.

wrapped sweets

2 gift rosettes

2 sparkly pipe cleaners

shiny tape

red and green crêpe paper

jokes

2 cardboard tubes

2 Fill the tubes with the wrapped sweets and add a joke.

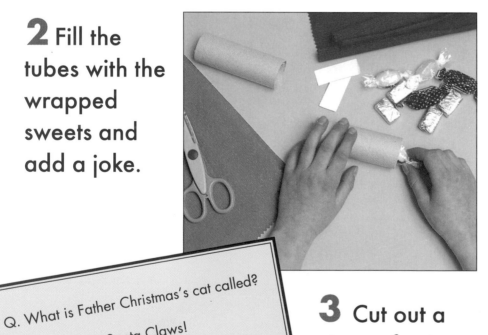

Q. What is Father Christmas's cat called?

A. Santa Claws!

3 Cut out a piece of crêpe paper in each colour the same width as in step 1 but 2 cm shorter. Centre the smaller pieces of crêpe paper on top of the larger pieces.

Did you hear about the Christmas robin for sale in the pet shop in January?

It was going cheap!

4 Place the cardboard tubes in the middle of the crêpe paper pieces. Wrap the paper around the tubes and secure with tape.

Knock! Knock!
Who's there?
Chris.
Chris who?
Christmas!

Q. What is Father Christmas's wife called?

A. Mary!

Q. Why is Rudolph's nose like a book?

A. Because they're both red!

5 Cut the pipe cleaners in half and twist around each end of the crackers to fasten.

6 Decorate each cracker with shiny tape and a gift rosette.

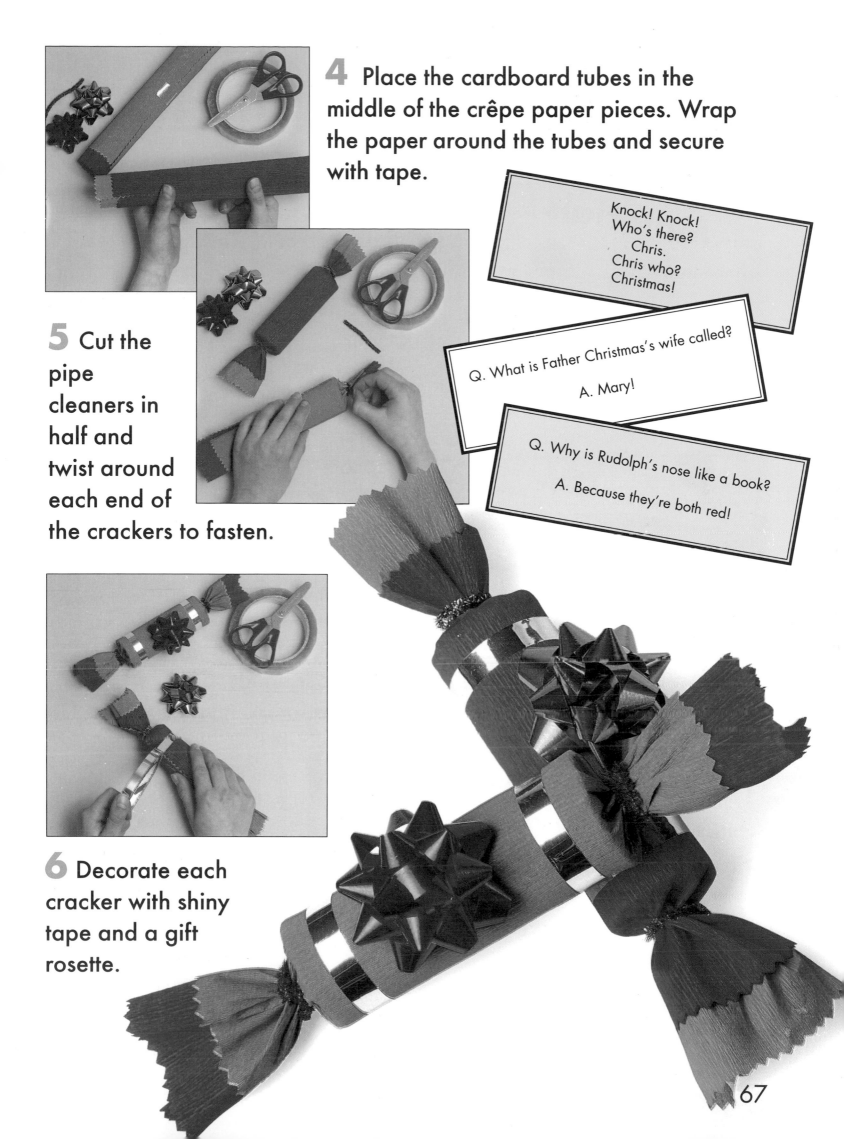

67

Truffle Puddings

Materials

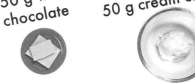

sweet cases

25 g cocoa powder

50 g white chocolate

50 g cream cheese

25 g chopped glacé cherries

25 g currants

edible cake decorations

50 g icing sugar

Gift wrap each truffle pudding in a homemade box (see page 77) and give as a present. This mix makes 7.

1 Put the cream cheese, icing sugar, cocoa powder, currants and cherries into the mixing bowl and stir well to mix them all together.

2 Roll into small balls between your hands. Chill in the fridge for 30 minutes.

⚠ **3** Melt the white chocolate in a heatproof bowl placed in a saucepan of simmering water. Put a blob of melted chocolate on top of each sweet.

4 Decorate with the edible cake decorations.

Snowballs

To avoid a snowball fight, make lots of these sweets! This mix makes 7.

Materials

100 g white chocolate

50 g cream cheese

sweet cases

50 g ground almonds

dessicated coconut

50 g icing sugar

1 Stir the cream cheese, icing sugar and ground almonds together in a bowl until well mixed.

Keep in the fridge and eat within a week

2 Roll into small balls between your hands.

! **3** Melt the white chocolate in a heat-proof bowl in a saucepan of simmering water. First roll the balls in the chocolate and then in the dessicated coconut.

Musical Greetings

Ring out a seasonal message with this simple-to-make card.

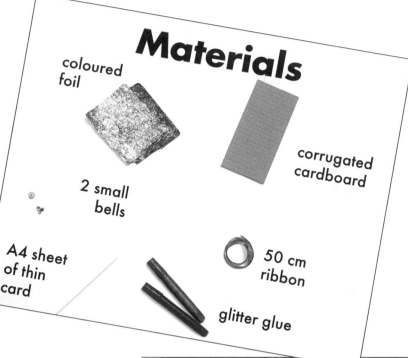

Materials

coloured foil

corrugated cardboard

2 small bells

A4 sheet of thin card

50 cm ribbon

glitter glue

1 Punch 2 holes in the top of the corrugated cardboard. Trace off the bell template on page 245, centre over a hole and transfer the outline. Repeat. Cut out the 2 bells.

2 Cover the cardboard bells with foil, and stick down with glue. Sew a real bell to the bottom of each.

3 Cut the piece of A4 card in half lengthways. Take one piece and fold in half. Make 3 holes along the folded edge with a hole punch. (You can use the other half to make another card later.)

70

4 Decorate the front of the card with a border using first felt-tip pens, then glitter glue.

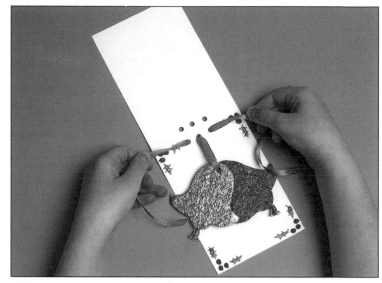

5 Thread the cardboard bells on to the ribbon. Open out the card and thread both ends of the ribbon through the centre hole. Thread each ribbon end back through the holes on either side and tie in a bow at the top.

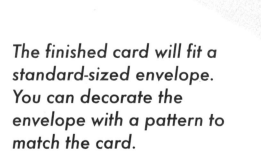

The finished card will fit a standard-sized envelope. You can decorate the envelope with a pattern to match the card.

71

Surprise, Surprise!

It's no great surprise to receive a card at Christmas, unless it's one of these!

Materials

2 sheets A4 thin white card

small piece of sponge

glitter glue

sticky shapes

Pop-up snowman

1 Cut one sheet of card in half widthways. Fold the 2 pieces of card in half again.

2 Decorate the inside of one of the pieces of card by sponging with blue and white paint. Leave to dry.

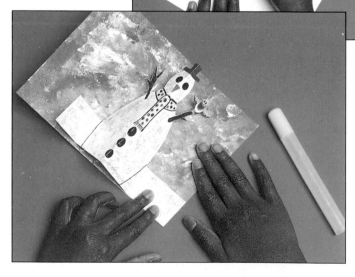

3 Trace off the snowman template on page 246 on to the outside of the other piece of card. Colour with felt-tip

4 Fold back the tabs on the snowman and glue to the bottom corners of the sponged card.

Expanding tree

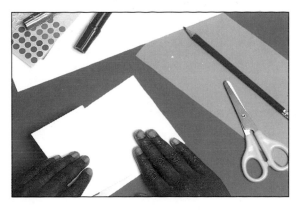

5 Cut a sheet of card in half lengthways. Fold one of the pieces in half. Now fold back one of the halves in half again. Open out.

6 Trace the tree template on page 246 on to the card taking care to position it correctly on the folds.

7 Paint and leave to dry. Decorate the tree with sticky shapes and glitter glue.

The finished cards. All that is left for you to do is to write on your own Christmas messages.

Materials

1 egg, beaten

boiled sweets broken into small pieces

liquorice laces

icing

2 teaspoons ground ginger

1 teaspoon ground cinnamon

cutters

gold and silver balls

100 g butter

4 tablespoons golden syrup

½ teaspoon bicardonate of soda

350 g plain flour

175 g soft brown sugar

Spicy Biscuits

This dough makes 35 biscuits. You'll find it easier to roll out in 2 halves.

1 Sieve the flour, spices and bicarbonate of soda into a large bowl.

2 Cut the butter into small chunks and rub in between your fingers until the mixture looks like fine breadcrumbs. Stir in the sugar.

[!] 3 Warm the syrup in a saucepan until it is runny. Put the syrup and the beaten egg

into the bowl and mix together. Gather the dough into a ball and knead well until it is smooth.

4 Roll out half the dough on a lightly-floured surface until it is about 5 mm thick. Cut shapes from the rolled dough. Use a small round bottle lid to cut out the centre of some of the biscuits.

74

! 5 Make a hole at the top of each biscuit. Place on a baking tray covered with greaseproof paper and bake in a preheated oven at 190°C/375°F/Gas Mark 5.

! 6 After 4 minutes take the biscuits out of the oven. Make the hanging hole bigger. Put broken pieces of boiled sweet in the centre holes.

! 7 Return to the oven and bake for about 6 minutes more. When the biscuits are completely cold, peel off the greaseproof paper. Decorate with the icing and gold and silver balls.

Thread a liquorice lace through each hole to hang the biscuits from the tree. Make the biscuits a few days before Christmas and keep them in an air-tight container. Hang them on the tree on Christmas Eve.

Three Tree Decorations

This year cover your Christmas tree with homemade decorations that sparkle and shine.

Silver bells

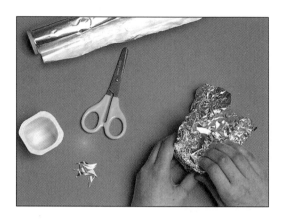

1 Trim around the edges of the yoghurt pots so that they are curved. Cover with foil.

2 Make a hole in the pots. Thread a bell on to each pipe cleaner. Twist the ends of the pipe cleaner together and push through the holes.

Foil snow flakes

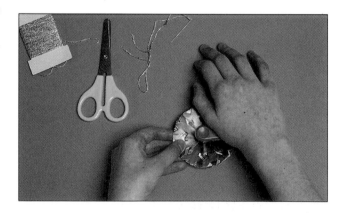

3 Cut 8 circles from double-sided foil. Fold 1 circle in half and half again and half again. Snip shapes from the edges of the folded paper circle. Repeat with the other 7 circles.

4 Open out the cut circles. Put them together and staple in the centre. Open out into a ball. Sew a thread to the top for hanging.

Present boxes

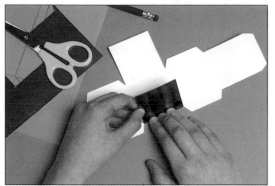

! **5** Trace off the template on page 246 on to the shiny side of the card and cut out. Score lightly along the lines and fold over.

6 Put glue on the side tabs and press firmly in place inside the box. Glue the top tab to the outside of the box. Tie ribbon around the box in a decorative bow for hanging.

The dressed tree. To make the felt stockings, see page 216, and for the decorated biscuits see page 74.

The silver bells can be hung up individually or twist the pipe cleaners together to hang them as a pair.

Lantern Chains

Light up your living room this Christmas with these sparkly lantern chains.

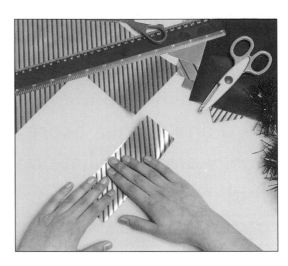

1 Cut a piece of paper 11 x 15cm and fold in half lengthways.

2 Use pinking shears to make snips along the folded edge about 1cm apart, leaving 1cm uncut along the unfolded edge. Open out the paper.

Join the lanterns to the chain by making one of the strips into a handle. Thread it through the chain, then glue either end of the strip and stick to the top of the lantern. Make sure you space the lanterns evenly along the chain.

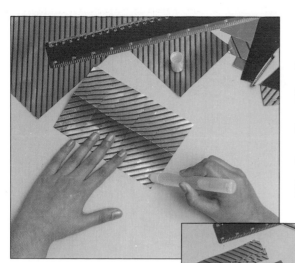

3 Put glue along a short edge. Curl the paper around and overlap the edges to stick together.

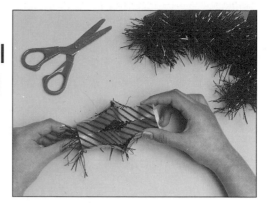

4 Cut a short piece of tinsel and push into the lantern to make a flame.

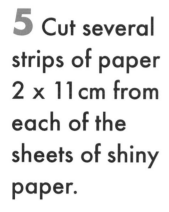

5 Cut several strips of paper 2 x 11cm from each of the sheets of shiny paper.

6 Make a loop with a strip and glue the ends together. Thread a different coloured strip through the loop and glue the ends together. Make the chain as long as you like.

All Chained Up

Materials

4 rolls of coloured crêpe paper

40 x 10 cm strip of brown paper

red and white sticky spots

You can make these chains as long as you need to fill your room.

Folded chains

1 Cut 3-cm wide strips from crêpe paper cutting through the whole roll. Glue 2 different-coloured strips together as shown in step 2. Leave to dry.

Concertina chain

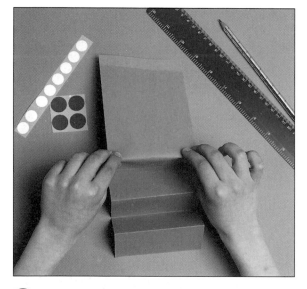

2 Fold the strips over one another, back and forth, until the whole length is folded. To make the chain longer glue another 2 strips to the ends and continue folding. Glue the ends together. Trim and leave to dry. Pull out and hang.

3 Fold the strip of light brown paper into a concertina, making folds every 5 cm.

4 Trace the reindeer template on page 246 on to the folded paper and cut out.

80

To make a star chain, cut out card stars (template page 245). Decorate with silver foil and sequins. Use curled gift ribbon to tie them on to ribbon.

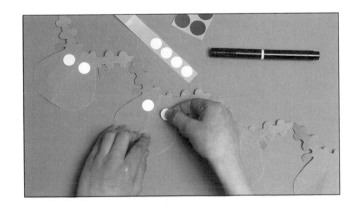

5 Unfold the paper. Stick the white dots on to each reindeer face to make the eyes.

6 Stick on the red dots to make noses. Finish off the mouth and eye details with a black felt-tip pen.

81

Robin Piñata

A Christmas party game that's fun for everyone.

Materials

corrugated cardboard

1 metre ribbon

large button

wrapped sweets

balloon

lolly stick

orange and brown card

black felt

newspaper strips

red and white tissue-paper

flour and water paste (see page 25)

⚠ 1 Blow up the balloon and tie the end in a knot. Cover the balloon with paste and stick the newspaper strips all over. Add another 5 layers and leave to dry in a warm place for 24 hours.

⚠ 2 Pierce the balloon at the top to let out the air. Remove the balloon. Mark and cut a large flap into the side of the papier mâché. Thread the ribbon through the hole at the top and pull out through the slit.

3 Make a hole in the centre of a corrugated cardboard circle and thread the ribbon through. Tie the lolly stick to the ribbon. Thread a large button on to the ribbon. Push the card circle back through the slit. Pull the ribbon up tight and tie in a knot at the top.

4 Fill with sweets.

5 Paint brown. When dry mark on the robin's red and white breast. Cut out red and white tissue-paper feathers and glue on to the robin.

6 Cut 2 wings from the brown card (template page 245) and glue on to either side. Cut 2 beaks and 2 feet from orange card (templates page 245) and glue in place. Add black felt circle eyes.

The finished robin makes a lovely decoration. When it's party time, hang the robin on a door frame. Your friends are blindfolded in turn and spun around. They try to hit the robin with a wooden spoon until it bursts scattering sweets across the floor.

83

Materials

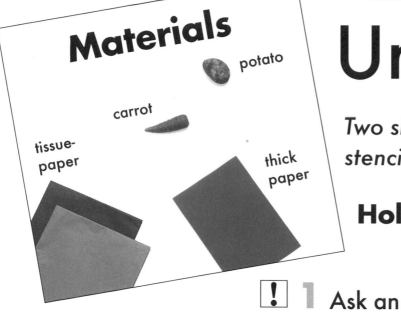

potato

carrot

tissue-paper

thick paper

Under Wraps

Two simple ideas for printing and stencilling your own wrapping paper.

Holly print paper

! **1** Ask an adult to cut a holly leaf shape from half a potato.

2 Dip the cut potato into green paint and print holly leaves on to tissue-paper.

Add sparkly detail to the wrapping paper with glitter and glitter glue.

3 Cut the end from a carrot. Dip into red paint and print berries next to the leaves.

Snow scene

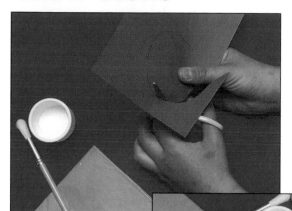

4 Draw a circle on to thick paper and cut out.

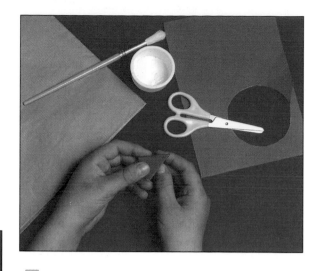

5 Fold the paper circle in half and half again and half again.

You can print matching gift tags on to folded card and attach to your presents with curled gift ribbon.

6 Cut out a pattern along the folded edges. Open out.

7 Use the cut circle as a stencil. Stencil white snowflakes on to coloured tissue-paper dabbing the paint over the cut areas.

85

Modelling

What you will need

Before you begin to make your models it is a good idea to get ready a few useful tools. You will need scissors for cutting; a pencil, eraser and ruler for drawing and marking out; glue for fixing things together; and paint and felt-tip pens for decorating. A light coat of varnish will give your models a shiny finish.

Kitchen Equipment

You will also need some standard kitchen tools including:

Measuring jug, mixing bowl, bucket, plastic bowl, measuring spoons, baking tray, greaseproof paper, cling film, chopping board, oven gloves, plastic spatula, wooden spoon, saucepan

petroleum jelly

ruler

pencil and eraser

felt-tip pens

poster paints

brushes

Other Useful Things

To cut and mark dough and clay
Plastic bottle tops, pen tops, jar lids, spoon handles, fork prongs, paper-clips, buttons, children's knitting needles, straws, pasta, cotton reels, garlic press, cocktail sticks

For plaster moulds
Any empty plastic food containers: yoghurt cartons, egg trays, chocolate box trays, etc.

To decorate your models
Material scraps, felt, pipe cleaners, glitter, straws, buttons, pasta, beads, seeds, sequins, ribbons, fir-cones, dried leaves and flowers, tree bark, shells, pebbles

hole punch

varnish or gloss

glue spreader

PVA glue

child's rolling-pin

cutters

modelling tool

scissors

Remember

☆ Wear an apron and cover the work area.
☆ Collect together the items in the materials box at the beginning of each project.
☆ Always ask an adult for help when you see this sign [!]
☆ Clear up after yourself.

Play Dough Fun

Play dough is quick and easy to make, but as it involves cooking you will need to ask a grown up to help you.

Materials

food colouring

100 g plain white flour

1 teaspoon cream of tartar

1 teaspoon cooking oil

150 ml water

50 g salt

1 Put the flour, salt, cream of tartar and cooking oil into a saucepan and stir together.

2 Add 1–2 teaspoonfuls of red food colouring to the water and stir well. The more you add the deeper the colour will be.

3 Gradually add the water to the other ingredients, mixing thoroughly to remove any lumps.

[!] **4** Cook over a low to medium heat. Stir continuously until the dough becomes thick and leaves the sides of the pan almost clean.

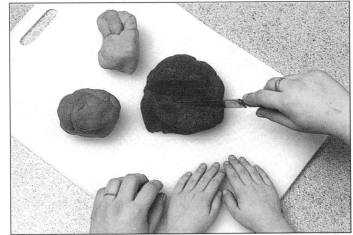

! 5 Scrape the mixture from the saucepan onto a smooth flat surface. Put the saucepan into soak immediately. Make up two more batches of blue and yellow play dough.

! 6 Leave the play dough to cool for at least ten minutes. Before using the dough ask an adult to cut through it with a knife to test that the inside has cooled too.

7 Knead the cooled play dough until it becomes smooth and pliable. You can mix the three colours to get a marbled effect.

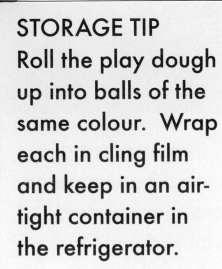

8 You can make up a variety of colours by mixing together red, yellow and blue.
Red and yellow makes orange.
Blue and yellow makes green.
Red and blue makes purple.

STORAGE TIP
Roll the play dough up into balls of the same colour. Wrap each in cling film and keep in an air-tight container in the refrigerator.

Play Dough Pictures

Roll out a ball of all the different coloured play dough you have made.

Materials

coloured card

coloured play dough

pipe cleaners

sequins

buttons

1 Cut out rectangles and squares from the rolled out play dough. Cut the squares in half to make triangles, and cut the triangles in half to make even smaller triangles.

2 Use bottle tops, jar lids and pastry cutters to cut out circles, ovals and crescent shapes.

3 Now start to put these shapes together onto backgrounds of coloured card to make pictures.

4 You can add detail to your pictures in all sorts of ways. A cotton reel pressed into a play dough circle makes great tractor wheels.

90

5 Use a cocktail stick to mark 'fur' onto a play dough animal.

6 A button bow tie and pipe cleaner whiskers finish off this cat *purr*fectly.

7 A paper-clip can be used to mark on bird feathers or fish scales.

You can have lots of fun putting the finishing touches to your picture.

91

Play Dough Bakery

Remember, although these things look good enough to eat they wouldn't taste nice at all, so please don't try it!

Iced cherry cakes

Materials

coloured play dough

plate

sweet cases

1 Roll some small and large balls of the red play dough and some medium-sized balls of the yellow play dough.

2 Flatten a yellow ball between your fingers and drape over a large red ball. Top with a small red ball.

Croissants

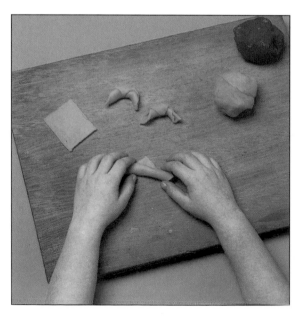

3 Roll out some yellow play dough until it is very thin. Cut into squares.

4 Roll up a square from one corner. Bend into a crescent shape.

Jam tarts

5 Roll out some yellow play dough to about ½ cm thick and cut out some circles with a small pastry cutter.

6 Press a small bottle top in the centre of each cut circle to make an indentation.

7 Place a ball of red or yellow play dough in the hollow and flatten to fill the space.

Why not try modelling a variety of fruits from your play dough, such as oranges, apples, cherries, grapes, bananas and pears. Use pipe cleaners to make stalks and leaves.

93

Salt Dough Medallions

Salt dough can be baked hard, painted and varnished so that you can keep the things you make forever.

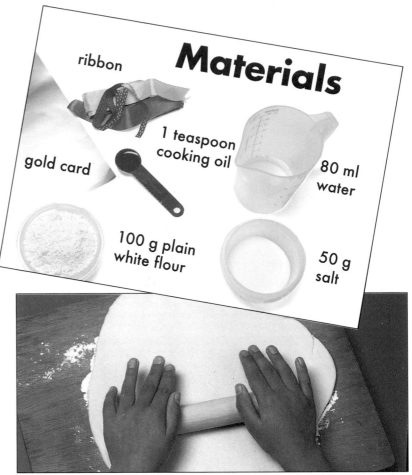

Materials

ribbon

gold card

1 teaspoon cooking oil

80 ml water

100 g plain white flour

50 g salt

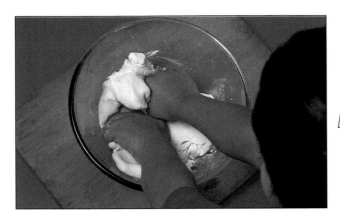

1 Mix together the salt, flour and cooking oil in a bowl. Add the water a little at a time and mix to a smooth paste that leaves the sides of the bowl clean.

3 Use pastry cutters to cut out several shapes from the salt dough.

2 Place the dough onto a lightly-floured board. Use a lightly-floured rolling-pin to roll out the dough to about ½ cm thick.

4 Use a paper-clip to print a pattern on the medallions.

! **5** Open out the paper-clip and prick out a circular pattern on the medallions. Place them onto a greased baking tray and bake in a pre-heated oven at 120°C until they are firm (about 2 hours).

! **6** Remove the medallions from the oven and leave to cool. Paint and lightly varnish. Decorate the medallions. To make a winning medal, cut a star from gold card and glue onto the centre of one of the medallions.

7 Overlap the ends of the ribbon and glue together. Stick the medallion firmly to the overlapped ends of the ribbon.

The medallions can easily be changed into badges by simply taping a safety pin to the back of the decorated shapes.

Materials

ribbon

salt dough

felt

2 pipe cleaners

material

Faces On the Door

Follow the instructions for making salt dough on page 94, then use it to model these jolly faces to hang over your bedroom door.

1 Lightly flour your hands and a board. Knead the dough on the board until it is smooth. Break off a small piece and put to one side.

2 Press the larger ball of dough into a face shape about 1 cm thick. To make the eyes and mouth twist a pencil into the face.

3 Break the remaining dough into two and shape a nose and a moustache. Use a little water to lightly wet the back of each piece and position onto the face.

! **4** Bake in a pre-heated oven on a greased baking tray at 120°C for 3-4 hours until firm. When cool, paint and varnish.

96

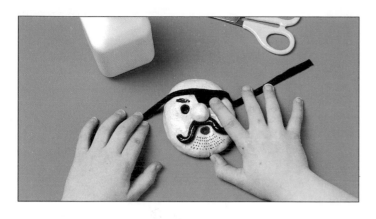

5 Cut an eye patch and band from the felt. Position on the face and secure with glue at the back of the head.

6 Make an earring by twisting a pipe cleaner into a circle. Glue to the side of the pirate's head.

7 Wrap the material around the pirate's head and secure on one side with the other pipe cleaner. Glue the finished head onto a long piece of ribbon.

Hang the completed faces over your cupboard or bedroom doors. You could model smaller faces and hang these from drawers.

A Christmas Decoration

To colour the salt dough, simply follow the recipe on page 94, but add 1 tablespoon of red food colouring to the mixing water.

Materials

glitter

wide red ribbon

red salt dough

narrow red ribbon

2 baubles

tinsel

florists' fine gauge wire

2 sprigs holly

1 On a lightly-floured board, roll the salt dough into a thick sausage shape about 30 cm long. Make a hole with a pencil at one end of the sausage and model the other end into a point.

!2 Place onto a greased baking tray and form into a circle. Moisten the pointed end and put into the hole. Smooth the join. Score the top of the ring with a plastic knife. Bake in a pre-heated oven for 3-4 hours at 120°C until firm, turning occasionally. Set aside to cool.

3 Lightly spread glue across the top of the dough circle and sprinkle on the glitter. Stick tinsel around the edge.

4 Thread the baubles onto the florists' wire. Twist the wire to keep them in place. Position the baubles on the bottom edge of the circle and secure by firmly winding the wire around the dough circle.

5 To hide the wire, wrap the wide ribbon between the baubles and tie into a bow. Glue the ends of the holly sprigs and tuck into the bow.

6 Thread the narrow ribbon through the top of the circle and knot to make a loop for hanging up the decoration. Tie the ribbon ends into a bow.

Pots of Fun

The models on the next few pages have been made using air-hardening clay. This will need to be left for a few days in a cool, dry place. But the end results will be well worth the wait!

1 Take 2 small lumps of clay and shape into balls between the palms of your hands.

2 Flatten the balls with your fingers.

3 Use a pastry cutter to cut out a circle from each for the base and the lid of the pot. Use a round-ended knife to cut away the rough edges of the circles.

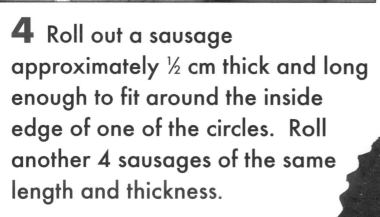

4 Roll out a sausage approximately ½ cm thick and long enough to fit around the inside edge of one of the circles. Roll another 4 sausages of the same length and thickness.

100

5 Trim each end of the sausages with a diagonal cut. Now wet and gently press together the ends of each sausage to make a perfect coil.

6 Place a coil on the inside edge of one of the circles. Build up the pot by wetting and placing the remaining coils on top of each other.

You can have lots of fun decorating the pots and the lids.

STORAGE TIP
Once opened you can stop the clay drying out by wrapping it in foil or cling film and storing it in a plastic bag.

7 To make the pot lid, roll a small ball of clay and place in the centre of the second circle. Leave the pot and lid to harden in a cool, dry place for several days. Paint and varnish.

A Woodland Scene

This collection of clay animals will bring a touch of nature to your bedroom. If you run out of clay, you could use salt dough instead.

The spider

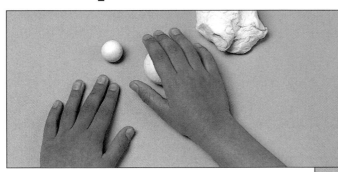

1 Roll out 2 balls of clay, a large one for the body and a small one for the head.

3 Use a cocktail stick to mark hairs over the body and the head.

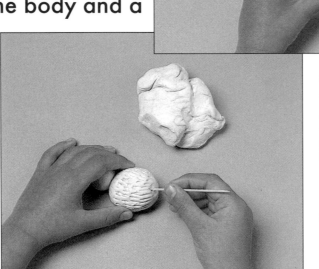

2 Push the spent matchstick into the body, leaving about 1 cm sticking out. Push on the head.

The ladybird

4 Take a small ball of clay and model it into a ladybird shape. Use a cocktail stick to mark in the head and the wings.

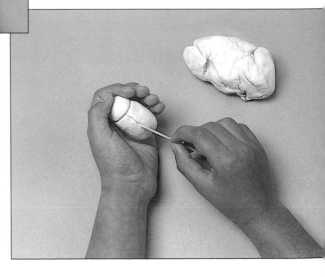

Materials

fir cones, leaves and tree bark

air-hardening clay

felt

glitter

spent matchstick

pipe cleaners

The snail

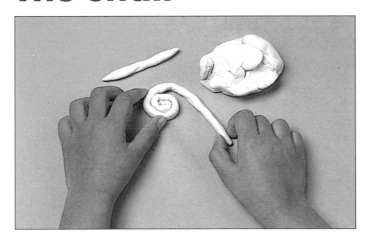

5 Roll a long and a short sausage from the clay. Roll up the long sausage into a coil and place on the shorter sausage.

6 Use a cocktail stick to mark in the snail's eyes and mouth, and to decorate the shell.

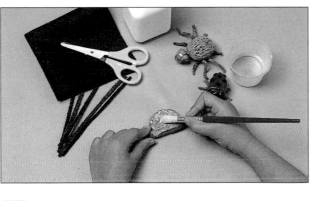

7 Leave the clay animals to dry out for several days, then paint and varnish them. Glue 8 pipe cleaner legs to the underside of the spider and 6 to the ladybird. Stick 8 black felt spots to the ladybird's back. Glue glitter on the spider's head.

Make a woodland scene on green card to display your clay animals. Decorate with stones, fir cones, leaves, dried flowers and tree bark

Lighthouse Picture

Make this super picture for your bedroom wall. You can use salt dough instead of clay if you prefer.

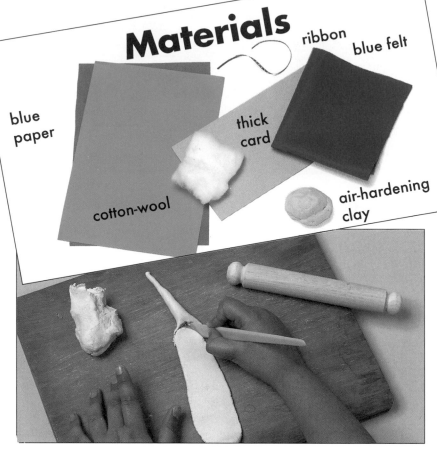

Materials

ribbon

blue felt

blue paper

thick card

cotton-wool

air-hardening clay

1 Roll some clay into a long sausage, thicker at one end than the other. Flatten using a rolling-pin.

2 Use a round-ended knife or modelling tool to cut out a lighthouse shape from the flattened clay.

3 Mark in the lantern house, windows and doors.

4 Shape the leftover clay into jagged rocks. Lay all the clay pieces onto a cling film-covered board and leave to harden for several days in a cool, dry place.

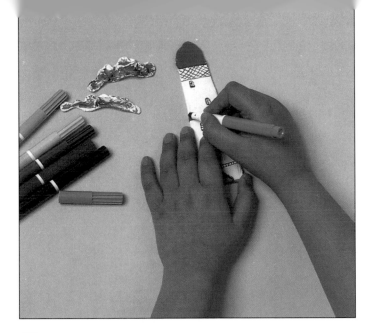

5 Paint the rocks brown and the lighthouse white. Once the paint has dried, use felt-tip pens to mark in details on the lighthouse.

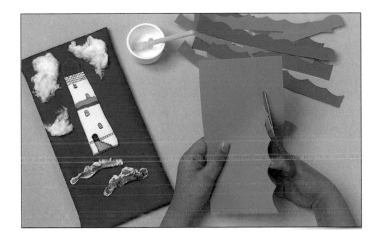

7 Cut wave shapes from blue paper and glue in place beneath the lighthouse and around the rocks. Stick cotton-wool clouds in the sky.

8 Punch 2 holes at the top of the card and thread a ribbon through for hanging up the picture.

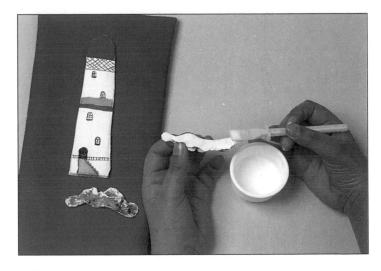

6 Cut a piece of card 28 cm x 14 cm and cover with the felt. Stick the lighthouse in the centre of the card. Position the rocks beneath the lighthouse and glue in place.

Cone People

Papier mâché simply means 'mashed paper'. You can model it into any shape with your hands or by applying it to a mould. But it is a messy business and rubber gloves may be a good idea.

Materials

- 200 ml water
- 2 heaped tablespoons plain white flour
- newspaper
- feather
- wool
- scraps of felt
- yellow felt

1 Tear the newspaper into lengths about 3 cm wide. Tear these strips again into small pieces about 3 cm square. Put into a container.

! 2 Cover the torn paper with hot water and leave to soak overnight.

3 Take handfuls of paper and squeeze the water out. Place the squeezed-out paper into another bowl. Empty the water from the container.

4 Put the flour in the mixing jug. Add the water slowly and mix to a smooth, creamy paste.

5 Put the squeezed paper back into the bucket a little at a time, mixing it with small amounts of paste until it becomes a smooth pulp. You may need to mix more paste.

6 Take a handful of papier mâché and work into a cone. Smooth the sides. Leave to dry in a warm, dry place for several days.

7 Paint the cone with 2 coats of bright paint. When dry, paint on the eyes, nose and mouth.

8 Glue some short strands of wool around the sides and back of the head, about 4 cm from the top of the cone. Cut out a felt hoop large enough to fit over the top of the cone just above the hair. Add a feather.

If you cannot make a cone shape, make one that is rounded at the top instead, just like the little red model on the end.

Papier Mâché Boat

A plastic bottle cut in half makes a perfect mould for making the hull of a boat from mashed paper.

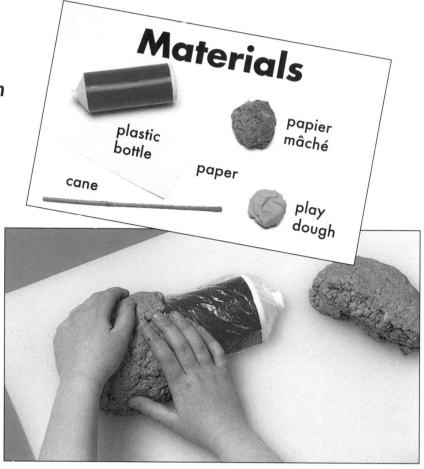

Materials

plastic bottle

papier mâché

paper

cane

play dough

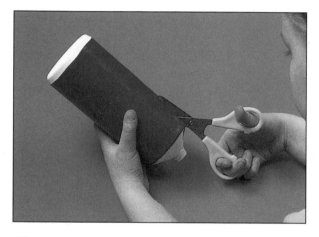

1 Cut a small plastic bottle in half lengthways. Cover one half with cling film.

2 Spread papier mâché evenly over the half bottle mould until it is about ½ cm thick. Leave to dry in a warm, dry place for several days.

3 Carefully ease the bottle and cling film from the papier mâché. Leave for a further day or two to let the inside dry out thoroughly.

4 Paint the boat inside and out. Several coats of paint may be needed. Once the paint has dried, the hull can be varnished.

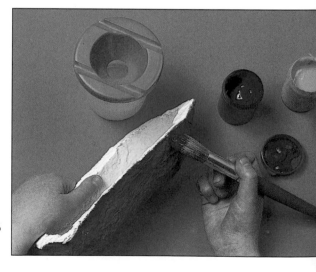

5 To make a sail, cut a piece of paper 24 cm x 20 cm and decorate with felt-tip pens.

6 Punch a hole at the centre top and centre bottom of the sail. Slip the sail onto the cane.

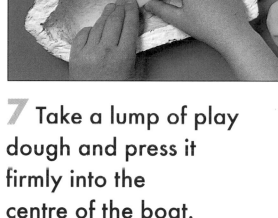

7 Take a lump of play dough and press it firmly into the centre of the boat. Push the cane mast into the play dough.

To make your boat into a Viking ship, cut out and decorate some circles for shields. Stick them along each side of the boat.

Papier Mâché Plate

Materials

2 heaped tablespoons plain white flour

small paper plate

newspaper torn into 3cm strips

100 ml water

magazine pictures

You can make this beautiful plate from just a few old newspapers and magazines.

1 Place the flour into a mixing jug. Gradually add the water to it to mix to a smooth, slightly runny paste.

2 Cover the front of the plate with petroleum jelly. Put a layer of newspaper strips on top. Paste well, smoothing down the paper with your fingers.

3 Lay a second layer of newspaper strips over the first layer, but in the opposite direction. Continue pasting and adding layers of newspaper strips first in one direction, then the other, until 8 layers have been completed.

4 Leave to harden for several days in a cool, dry place. When completely dry, remove the papier mâché carefully from the plate. Trim the edge with scissors to neaten.

To make this sun mobile, cut the edges of the papier mâché plate into sun ray shapes. Add a circle of beads and buttons to the centre and glue firmly in place. Spray the front and back with gold paint.

5 Paint the back of the plate. You may need several coats to cover the newspaper.

6 Decorate the front of the plate by gluing on magazine pictures.

7 Paint a light varnish over the finished plate.

Materials

modelling plaster

play dough

cocktail sticks

felt

dried flowers

thin white card

yoghurt carton

egg tray

Odds and Ends

Think twice before throwing away any plastic packaging from food products. All make excellent moulds for plaster casting. Here are some simple ideas for you to try out.

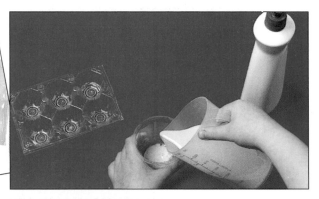

1 Wipe the insides of the plastic moulds with washing-up liquid, and fill with modelling plaster. Leave to harden, then carefully remove from the moulds.

Windmill

2 Paint the yoghurt cast white and an egg cast red. When this has dried, paint in doors and windows on the yoghurt cast. Glue the egg cast to the top of the yoghurt cast.

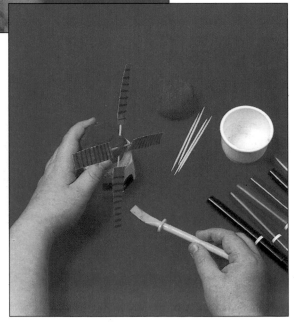

3 Cut out 4 sails from white card and decorate. Glue to the cocktail sticks and attach to the front of the windmill with play dough.

Party Place Names

4 Paint the remaining 5 egg casts in bright colours and leave to dry. Glue felt leaves and a dried flower to the top of each.

5 Write the names of your friends or family onto small rectangles of white card and stick to the bottom of each decorated cast.

Handprint Paperweight

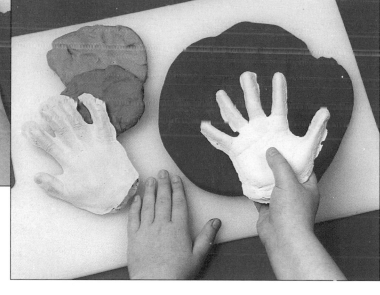

6 Roll out a large ball of play dough to about 1 cm thick. Firmly press your hand into the play dough. Fold up the bottom edge of the play dough if it has become flattened out. Fill the mould with plaster and leave to dry for several hours.

7 Carefully peel away the play dough from the plaster cast. Paint and varnish. Use the plaster hand to keep your drawings in place and store paper-clips in the palm.

Beads, Badges & Bangles

What you will need

Before you begin to make jewellery it is a good idea to get ready a few useful tools. You will need a pencil, eraser and ruler for drawing and marking out, and a compass is handy for measuring perfect circles. For cutting paper, thin card or fabric, you can use a pair of round-ended scissors or pinking shears, but you will need to ask a grown up to cut thick card for you with a craft knife. You can use glue or tape to fix things together, and you will need a needle and thread ready for sewing. Paint and felt-tip pens are needed for decorating. Some of the finished projects will need a light coat of varnish.

modelling tool

PVA glue and spreader

paint

felt-tip pens

paint-brushes

needles

double-sided tape

pins

masking tape

rolling-pin

clear tape

Other Useful Things

All sorts of things come in useful for making jewellery. Start a collection and keep adding to it. Store useful odds and ends in a box. Your collection might include:

Plastic bottles, textured plastic packaging, cardboard tubes, yoghurt cartons, bottle tops, jar lids, old newspapers, corrugated cardboard, coloured card and coloured paper, gold and silver card, gummed paper, crêpe paper, tissue-paper, wool, string, gold and silver thread, elastic, cellophane and foil sweet wrappers, broken bead necklaces, tinsel, glitter, self-adhesive stickers, buttons, sequins, felt, material off-cuts, hair slides, hairbands, safety pins.

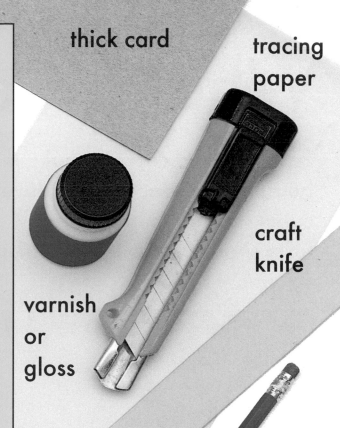

thick card

tracing paper

craft knife

varnish or gloss

compass

scissors

metal ruler

pencil and eraser

thread

pliers

pinking shears

Remember

☆ Wear an apron and cover the work area.
☆ Collect together the items in the materials box at the beginning of each project.
☆ Always ask an adult for help when you see this sign ⚠
☆ Clear up after yourself.

ruler

115

What a Corker!

Save up used corks to make this beautiful necklace. Alternatively corks can be bought cheaply from shops that sell wine-making equipment.

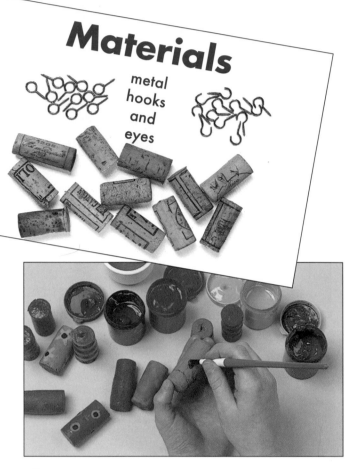

Materials

metal hooks and eyes

12 corks

1 Hold the corks at each end and paint using about 3 different base colours. Stand the painted corks on one end, paint the other end and leave to dry. Turn over and paint the other end the same colour.

2 Decorate the painted corks with patterns in contrasting colours making them as bright as you can. Leave to dry.

3 Lightly varnish the painted corks and leave to dry.

4 Screw a hook and an eye into either end of 9 of the corks.

5 Join these 9 corks together. Use pliers to close up the hooks, but leave the last hook open so that the necklace can be put on easily.

6 Make a pendant by joining together the remaining 3 corks. Hook the pendant onto the necklace.

TO MAKE THE BRACELET
Cut several corks into 3 pieces each. Paint and varnish. Thread a piece of wool or thin elastic through a darning needle. Push the needle through the centre of a cork bead, thread on a brightly-coloured wooden bead, add another cork bead, then another wooden bead, and so on until the bracelet is long enough to fit your wrist. Unthread the needle and tie the ends of elastic into a knot, and trim back the ends.

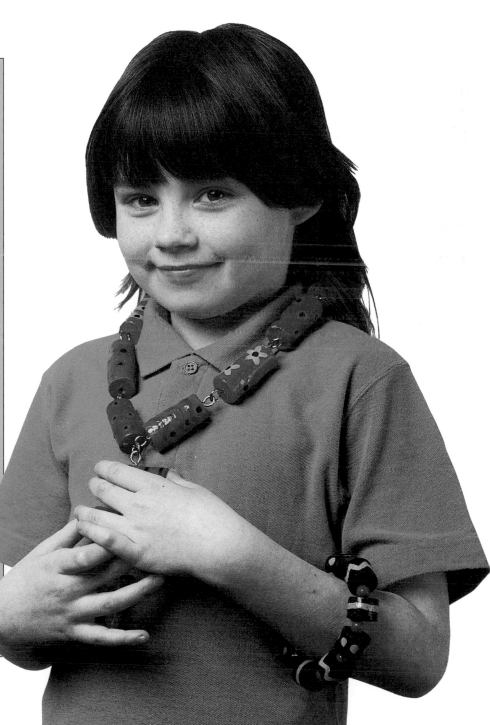

Robot Badges

An opportunity to use lots of bits and pieces – collect anything silver and gold and create your own robotic characters.

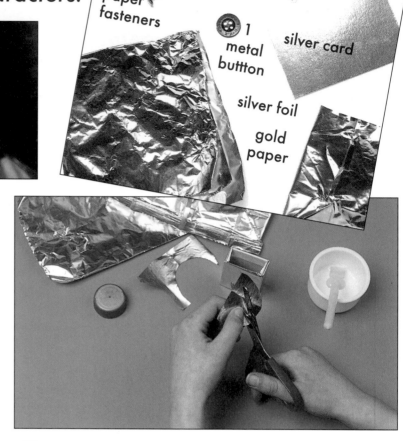

1 Cover a matchbox with silver foil leaving one end unwrapped. Pull down the cardboard flap at the open end and cut off. Push the matchbox back in.

2 Cut a semi-circle of gold paper. Cut a fringe along the curved edge.

3 Glue the fringed semi-circle onto the back of the bottle cap. Stick 2 sequins inside the bottle cap to make the robot's eyes.

4 Push the bottle cap head firmly into the open end of the matchbox.

! 5 Use a scissor blade to make a small slit a third of the way down each side of the matchbox. Push a long paper fastener into each hole to make the robot's arms.

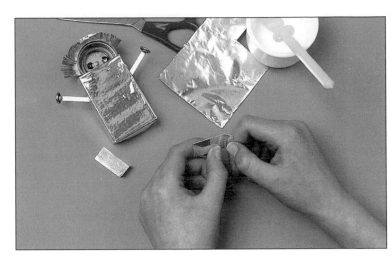

6 To make the robot's legs cut 2 pieces of thin silver card 1 cm x 3 cm and fold over 1 cm to make the feet. Glue to the back of the matchbox.

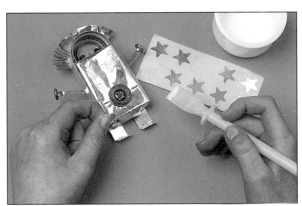

7 Decorate the front of the robot with the stars, sequins and button.

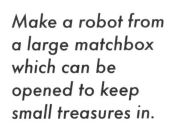

8 Tape a safety pin to the back of the robot and it is ready to wear.

Make a robot from a large matchbox which can be opened to keep small treasures in.

119

Bottle Bracelets

Recycle plastic bags and bottles to make these stunning bracelets. Wash out the bottles thoroughly first, and soak off the labels in warm, soapy water.

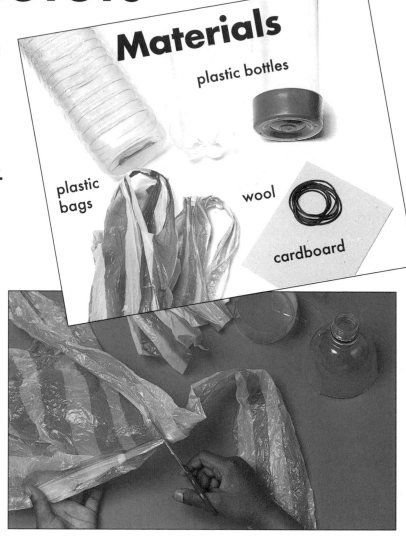

Materials

plastic bottles

plastic bags

wool

cardboard

! **1** Cut a 4-cm wide band from a round plastic bottle. Trim the edges with scissors. Try it on over your hand – if it is too big, cut and re-join with tape to fit.

2 Cut a plastic bag into strips roughly 5 cm wide.

3 Wind the strips around the plastic band securing each piece with a small piece of tape, until the bracelet looks well-padded.

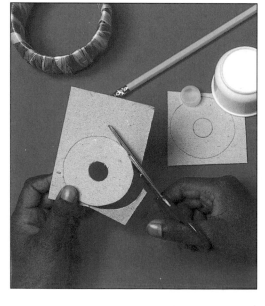

4 To make the pom pom, cut 2 discs from cardboard measuring 5 cm in diameter with a 1.5 cm hole in the centre.

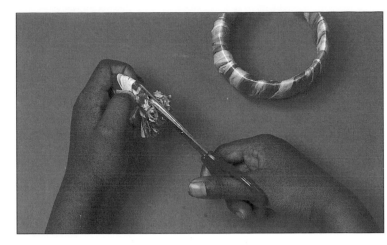

5 Cut striped plastic bags into thin strips. Wrap these around the card 'doughnut' until there are several layers of plastic covering it.

6 Use a pair of scissors to cut through the plastic along the edge of the cardboard rings.

7 Tie a long piece of wool securely around the plastic between the 2 cardboard rings and knot tightly. Cut through the cardboard rings and remove. Fluff up the pom pom and tie it onto the bottle bracelet. Trim off the ends of the wool.

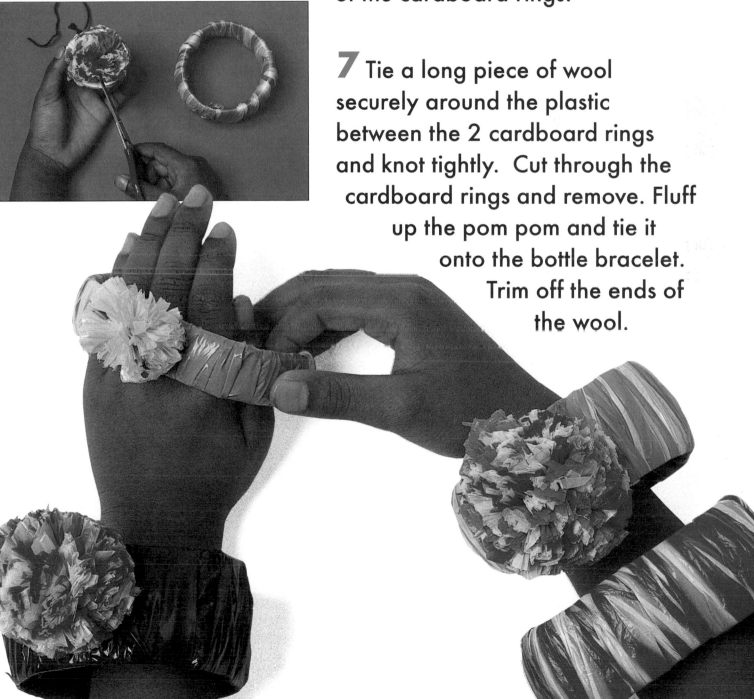

Autumn Leaf Necklace

A *super seasonal necklace made from bits of card and a few beads.*

Materials

9 wooden beads

corrugated cardboard

wool

1 Trace off the leaf templates on page 247 and draw 3 of each onto the corrugated card. Cut out.

2 Paint the leaves on both sides, using about 3 different base colours. Leave to dry.

3 Paint vein patterns onto the leaves in contrasting colours and leave to dry.

4 Lightly varnish the leaves on one side. Leave to dry, then turn over and varnish the other side.

5 Thread some wool onto a darning needle, making sure that it is long enough to go over your head. Push the needle through the back of the leaf close to the top edge. Thread on a bead, then push the needle back out through the front of the leaf.

6 Continue to thread on the leaves and the beads. When they are all threaded on, make sure there is an equal amount of wool left at each end and knot the ends together.

You could also make a summer shell necklace using the templates on page 247, threaded together with pearls rather than beads.

Materials

12 large pasta tubes

red and yellow card

feathers

8 beads

self-adhesive dots

large plastic pot with rim

black and white string

Apache Fun

A tooth necklace and feather armband that are perfect for dressing up.

Tooth necklace

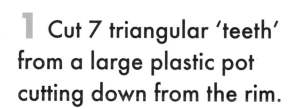

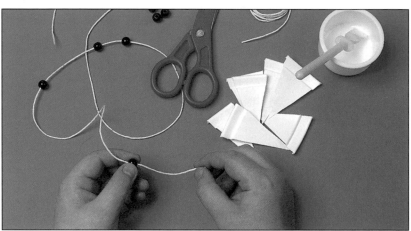

1 Cut 7 triangular 'teeth' from a large plastic pot cutting down from the rim.

2 Thread the beads onto a long piece of string. Run some glue under the rim of a tooth and stick onto the string between the middle 2 beads.

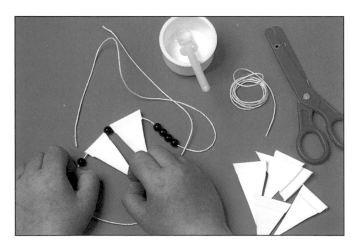

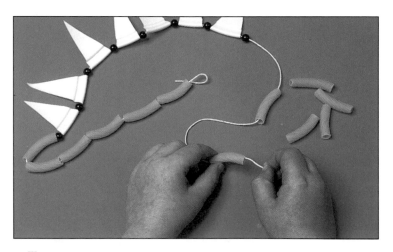

3 Continue to stick the teeth between the beads until they have all been used.

4 Thread 6 large pasta tubes onto either side of the string and knot the ends of the string together.

Feather armband

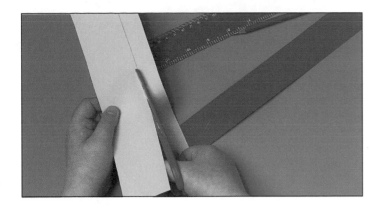

5 Cut a piece of red card 4 cm wide and long enough to go around your upper arm including a 4 cm overlap. Cut a strip of yellow card the same length and 2 cm wide.

6 Use pinking shears to cut out a zig zag along one edge of the yellow card and glue onto the red card. Stick black dots on each of the yellow triangles.

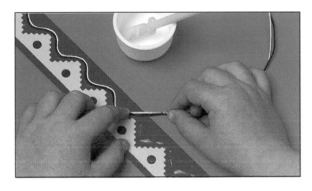

7 Cut off a long piece of black and white string and glue them onto the red card, following the zig zag pattern of the yellow card. Turn the card over and tape feathers along the bottom (string) edge.

You could make a feather headband too. Use double-sided tape to fix the headband and armband in place.

Snake Charmers

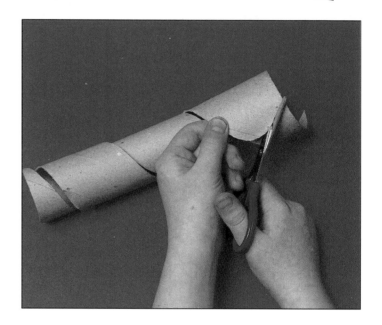

Materials

self-adhesive dots

2 sequins

white card

gummed paper

large cardboard tube

Sssssensational snakes to slither up your arms or hook over your ears.

Snake armband

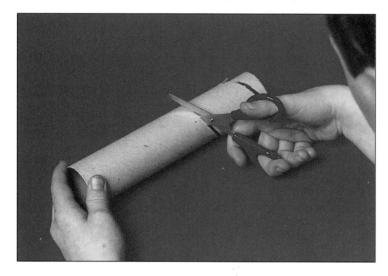

1 Cut the cardboard tube into a spiral about 5 cm wide. Straighten out gently and neaten the edges with scissors.

2 Cut one end rounded for the head. Leave the other end pointed for the tail.

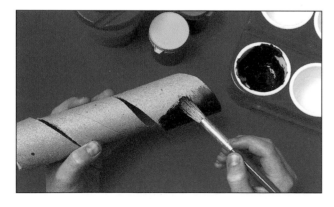

3 Paint the outside of the spiral green and leave to dry.

4 Tear the gummed paper into strips and use to

decorate the spiral. Fold the ends of the paper over the edges of the card.

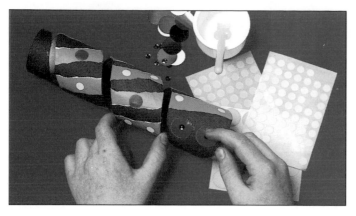

5 Stick small dots all over the snake's body to decorate. Stick 2 large dots onto the head for eyes and glue sequins into the centre of them.

Ear snake

6 Trace off 2 snakes onto white card using the template on page 247. Cut out and paint.

7 Decorate with self-adhesive dots.

You can wear the finished snake on your lower or upper arm. Hook the snake earrings over your ears.

Robin Hood Pouch

A simple-to-make money bag that can be hung from your belt or around your neck.

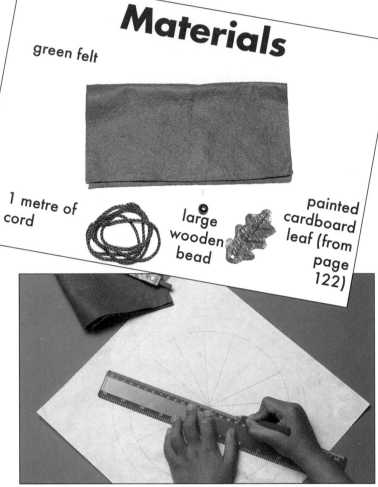

1 Use a compass to draw a 24-cm diameter circle onto a piece of paper. Draw another circle within it of 20 cm diameter.

2 Divide the inner circle up into 16 equal sections.

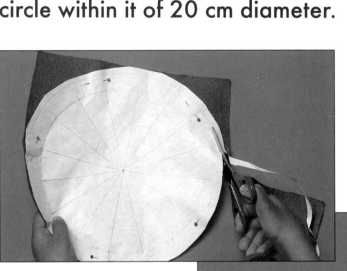

3 Roughly trim down the paper around the circle and pin onto the felt. Cut around the outer circle.

4 Before unpinning the paper, poke a pin through each of the 16 points marked on the inner circle and mark with a pen dot on the felt. Unpin the paper.

128

5 Fold in half along each of the marked dots in turn and cut tiny slits, just large enough to thread the cord through to make a drawstring.

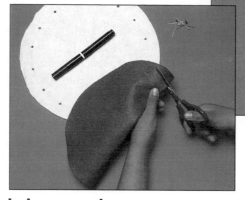

6 Begin to thread the cord through the holes. Thread on the painted leaf *(instructions for making on page 122)* between the 8th and the 9th hole.

7 When you have threaded the cord through all the holes, pull the ends together and ease the felt into a pouch shape.

8 Thread the cord ends through a snugly-fitting bead and knot the ends together. To close the pouch push the bead down.

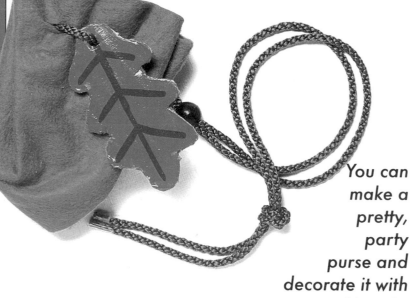

You can make a pretty, party purse and decorate it with sequins and beads.

Badges For Everyone!

These bright badges are made from layers of newspaper pasted onto a shaped card.

Materials

corrugated cardboard

silver foil

water and flour paste (page 25)

sequins and self-adhesive jewels

safety pins

newspaper

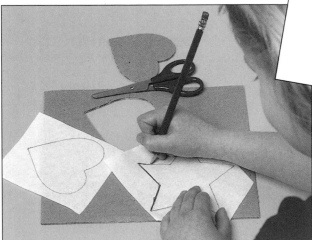

1 Trace off the heart and star templates on page 247 onto corrugated card, and cut out.

The sheriff star

3 Cover the star in silver foil, pressing carefully around the edges and gluing in place at the back.

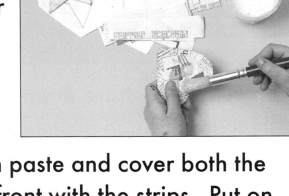

2 Tear the newspaper into short, thin strips. Brush the shapes lightly with paste and cover both the back and front with the strips. Put on several layers of newspaper strips, pasting in between. Leave to dry.

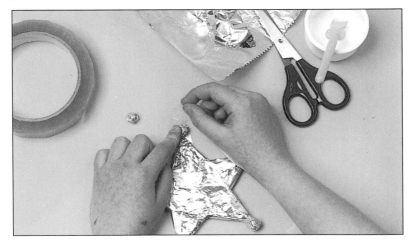

4 Roll 5 balls of foil and attach to the star points with tape.

The heart

5 Add more layers of newspaper to the centre of the heart to give a ballooning effect. Leave to dry.

6 Paint the base colour. When this is dry, paint on patterns in contrasting colours. Once dry cover with a light coat of varnish.

7 Once the varnish has dried, stick on jewels and sequins to decorate.

Tape safety pins to the back of the finished badges and they are ready to wear. You can also use the smaller templates on page 247 to make beautiful brooches. Decorate in the same way as the badges and tape gold thread between the decorated shapes.

131

Out of This World

Re-use old plastic bottles and packaging for effects that are out of this world.

The badge

1 Cut a circle from the metallic paper to fit snugly into the plastic lid. Secure with a dab of glue.

safety pin

self-adhesive stars

plastic lid with lip

silver spray paint

paper fastener

white paper

metallic paper

moulded plastic

2 large plastic bottles

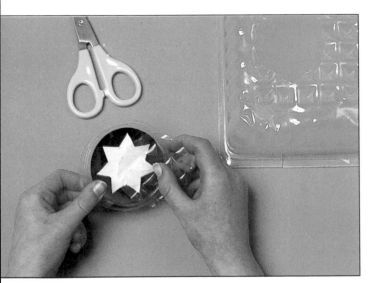

3 Cut a circle from the moulded plastic to fit snugly into the plastic lid and place on top of the star.

2 Cut a star out of white paper and stick in the centre of the metallic paper.

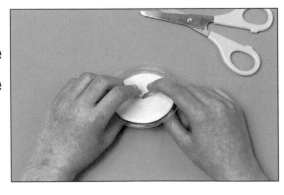

! 4 Pierce a hole in the centre of your junk sandwich with the end of a scissor blade. Push the paper fastener through the hole and open out at the back.

132

The gauntlets

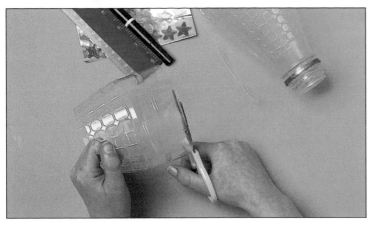

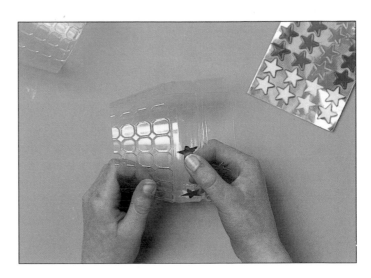

⚠**5** Mark 2 lines 7.5 cm and 15 cm from the neck of the bottles. Cut along these lines and trim the rough edges with scissors.

6 Stick two rows of stars around the wider end of the bottles.

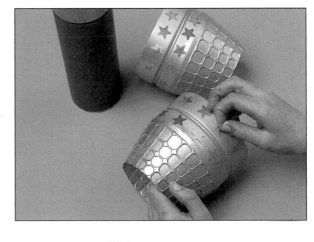

Tape a safety pin to the back of the badge and pin it onto your top. Slip the gauntlets over your hands and prepare for blast off.

7 Spray all over with silver spray paint. When the paint has dried completely carefully remove the stars.

133

Sparkly Garland

Don't just decorate the tree this Christmas. Why not decorate yourself too?

Materials

silver and red tinsel

thin gold ribbon

1 metre gold string

1 Cut 5 10-cm lengths from the silver tinsel and 5 10-cm lengths from the red tinsel. Cut 10 2-cm lengths of double-sided tape.

2 Fold each piece of tinsel in half and press a piece of double-sided tape onto it.

3 Attach a piece of silver tinsel 25 cm in from the end of the gold string by removing the backing from the double-sided tape and folding the tinsel around the string. Position all the silver tinsel pieces along the string about 10 cm apart from each other.

4 Cut 8 30-cm lengths from the gold ribbon. Tie 2 pieces onto the gold string between each piece of silver tinsel.

5 Push the gold ribbon close to the tinsel. Curl the ribbon with closed scissor blades.

Stick coloured tinsel onto hair slides, combs and hairbands to make some stunning sparkly bits for your hair.

6 Finally add the red tinsel pieces. Remove the backing of the double-sided tape and fold onto the gold string between the gold ribbons.

7 Knot the ends of the string together.

Animal Badges

These animal badges are made from salt dough, which can be modelled into any shape you choose.

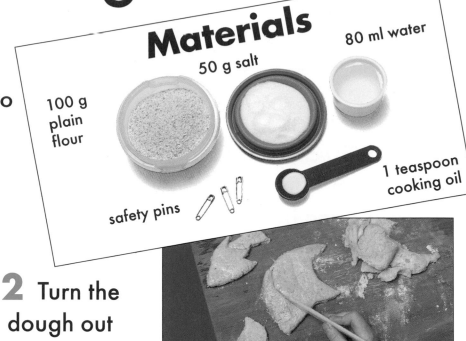

Materials

100 g plain flour

50 g salt

80 ml water

safety pins

1 teaspoon cooking oil

1 Mix together the salt, flour and cooking oil in a bowl. Add the water a little at a time and mix to a smooth paste.

2 Turn the dough out onto a lightly-floured board. Knead and roll out to about ½ cm thick. Cut out some animal shapes.

3 Add salt dough eyes, wings or fins. Model the dough, brush lightly with a little water and press down firmly onto the animal shapes.

! **4** Add decorative details. Place the finished badges onto a lightly-greased baking tray and bake in the oven on the lowest setting overnight.

5 Paint the animal shapes in bright colours and leave to dry.

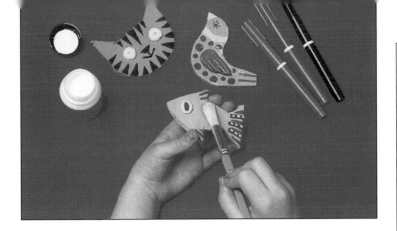

6 Add detail with a fine paint-brush, or felt-tip pens. Once dry, seal all over with a light coat of varnish.

Tape a safety pin to the back of the badges and they are ready to wear.

ANIMAL WALLHANGING
Make some other animal shapes – why not try zoo animals this time. Decorate and varnish them and glue them to a long piece of felt. Hang it up in your room.

Flowers For Your Hair

A corsage that will stay as fresh as the day you make it.

Materials

crêpe paper (dark pink, pink, yellow, green)

green wire

safety pin

1 Mark out circles measuring about 10 cm in diameter onto the crêpe paper. You will need 6 yellow and a total of 9 light and dark pink circles. Cut out. You can use pinking shears for decorative effect.

2 Place 3 circles of crêpe paper on top of each other. Fold in half. Hold in the centre and pinch together between thumb and forefinger.

3 Wind about 10 cm of wire around the base of the flower head. Twist the ends together and press close to the flower.

4 Cut a 5-cm wide strip of green crêpe paper. Cut a zig zag pattern along one edge to make the leaves. Cut into sections of 4 leaves long.

138

5 Wind a leaf section around the base of the flower head and secure with the end of a 15-cm length of wire. Leave the rest of the wire hanging down.

6 Cover the top of the wire with a piece of green crêpe paper 4 cm x 2 cm backed with double-sided tape: remove the backing and wind around pressing firmly together.

7 Once you have made all 5 flowers, hold together in a bunch. Wind the stem of one flower around the rest to keep in place.

Attach the bunch of flowers to a hat or a piece of clothing with a safety pin fastened inside the item of clothing. Individual flowers can be wound around a hairband or hair comb for a very pretty effect.

Masks

What you will need

Many of the masks in this chapter are made using the templates on pages 248-251, so do make sure that you have tracing paper. Also you will need a pencil, eraser and ruler for drawing and marking out, and a pair of compasses for measuring perfect circles. For cutting paper and thin card, you can use a pair of round-ended scissors, but you will need to ask a grown up to cut thick card for you with a craft knife. You will need glue or tape to fix things together, and paint and felt-tip pens for decorating the finished masks.

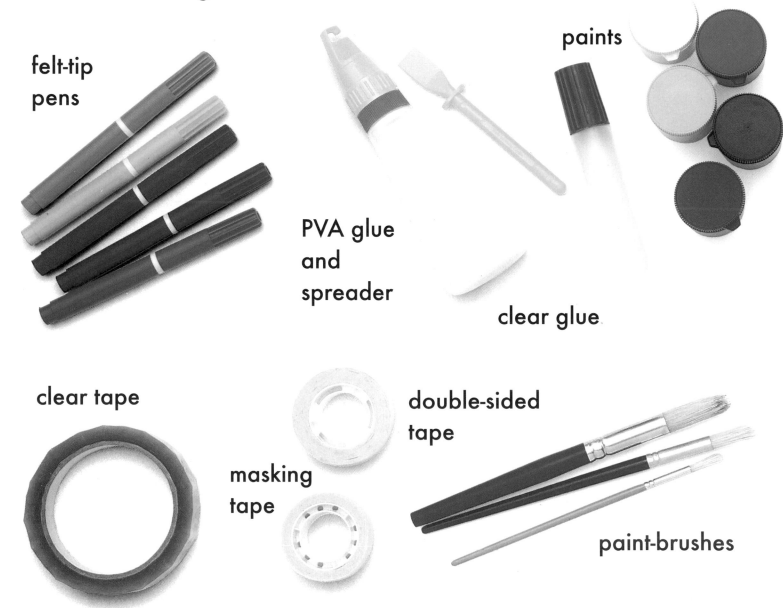

paints

felt-tip
pens

PVA glue
and
spreader

clear glue

clear tape

double-sided
tape

masking
tape

paint-brushes

Other Useful Things

All sorts of things come in useful for making masks. Start a collection and keep adding to it. Store useful odds and ends in a box. Your collection might include:

Textured plastic packaging, colourful plastic bags, cardboard tubes, yoghurt cartons, bottle tops, jar lids, old newspapers and magazines, corrugated cardboard, gold and silver card, coloured card and paper, gummed paper, crêpe paper, tissue-paper, wool, string, cellophane and foil sweet wrappers, broken bead necklaces, tinsel, glitter, sticky shapes, buttons, sequins, felt, fabric scraps, pasta, raffia, garden sticks, pipe cleaners.

thick card

craft knife

metal ruler

scissors

pencil and eraser

pair of compasses

tape measure

bradawl

toothbrush

Remember
☆ Wear an apron and cover the work area.
☆ Collect together the items in the materials box at the beginning of each project.
☆ Always ask an adult for help when you see this sign !
☆ Clear up after yourself.

ruler

Bag Monster

To make this giant mask you'll need a large paper carrier bag with side and bottom gussets.

Materials

red card

coloured paper

corrugated cardboard

large paper carrier bag

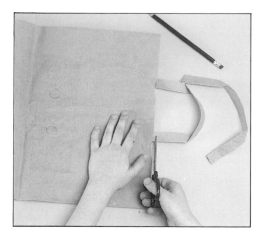

! **1** Put the bag over your head and ask an adult to draw on 2 small circles where your eyes are. Take the bag off and cut out the eye holes. Cut the handles off the bag.

2 Paint a frightening face on to the front of the bag. Leave to dry.

3 Cut 2 ears from the corrugated cardboard and decorate. Leave to dry.

4 Make a slit in the mouth. Cut a long tongue from red card, just wide enough to push through the monster's mouth.

5 Tape the ears to the side gussets of the bag.

6 Cut the coloured paper into strips of different lengths and widths. Curl by pulling firmly along closed scissor blades. Glue the curled paper all over the bag.

To give your friends a double fright paint a face on the back of the mask too.

143

Sunbeam

A golden mask to make you shine.

Materials

tinsel

corrugated cardboard

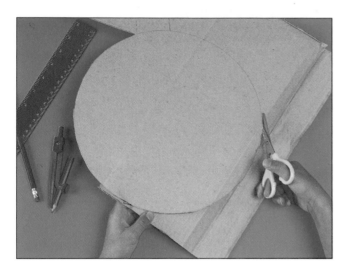

1 Draw a 28 cm-diameter circle on to the cardboard. Mark on a handle measuring 10 x 5 cm. Cut out.

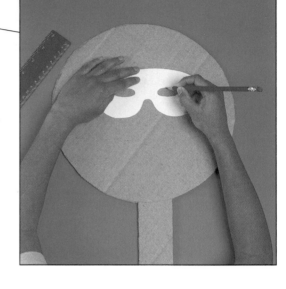

2 Use template A on page 248 to trace off the position of the eyes on the circle about a third of the way down. Cut out.

3 Cut triangles from cardboard. You will need enough to go all the way around the edge of the circle.

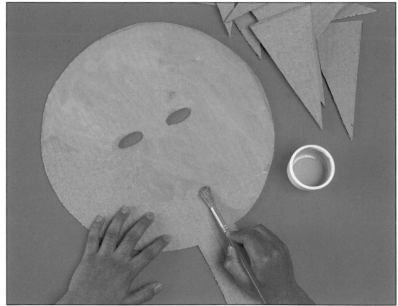

4 Paint the circle and the triangles yellow on one side. Leave to dry.

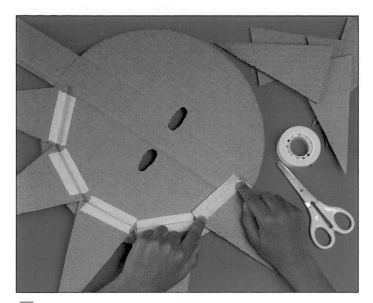

5 Tape the triangles to the unpainted side of the mask.

6 Paint a face on the front of the mask. Once the paint has dried glue tinsel around the face.

All that you need to make this stunning hand-held mask is corrugated cardboard and a bit of tinsel.

145

Mask on a Stick

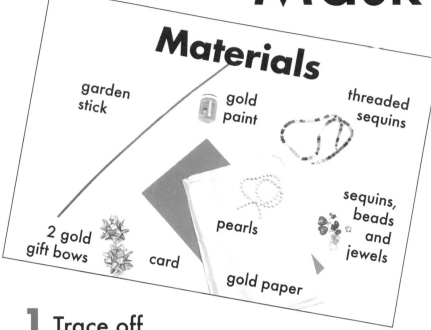

Materials

garden stick

gold paint

threaded sequins

2 gold gift bows

pearls

card

sequins, beads and jewels

gold paper

You can use all sorts of bits and pieces to decorate these simple-to-make eye masks.

1 Trace off template C on page 249 on to thick card to make a reuseable template. Draw around this template on to card and cut out. Stick the mask on to the gold paper and trim around the edges. Cut out the eye holes.

2 Decorate the front of the mask with the sequins, jewels, beads and pearls.

3 Stick a gold gift bow to each corner.

146

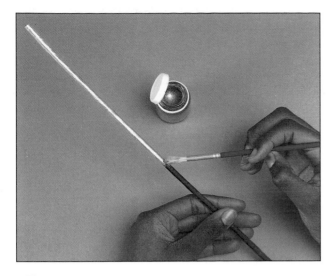

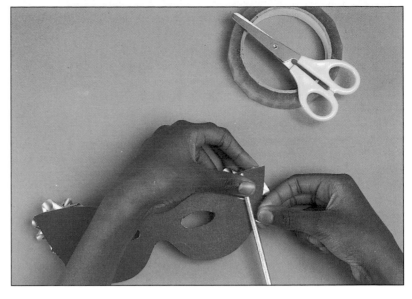

4 Cut the garden stick to about 30 cm long. Paint gold and leave to dry.

5 Tape the stick to one side on the back of the mask.

The finished mask! The other mask shown has been decorated with plastic flowers and a plastic beetle left over from a Christmas cracker. Butterflies have been cut from coloured paper and taped to plastic-covered wire.

An eye mask simply decorated with flashes of foil.

147

Reindeer

A fun mask to make for Christmas.

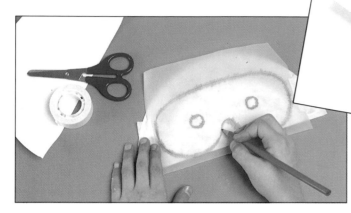

card

paper plate

thin elastic

1 Cut the plate in half. Tape a tracing of template B (page 248) to the rounded side of the plate. Draw around the eye holes and the bottom outline of the mask. Remove the tracing paper and cut out.

2 Paint the rounded side of the plate brown. Leave to dry.

3 Cut 2 ears from the card (template page 249). Paint brown and leave to dry, then paint the centre of the ears pink.

4 Trace off the antler template on page 249. Cut 2 from the card and paint both sides red. Leave to dry.

5 On the unpainted side of the mask, glue the antlers to the top and the ears to each side.

6 Make a small hole on either side of the mask. Tie a double knot at one end of a piece of elastic. From the front of the mask, thread the elastic through one hole to the other and secure with a double knot.

Spread a little Christmas cheer with this reindeer mask.

Christmas Tree Mask

Stick 2 card Christmas trees to the back of the mask. Decorate the trees with gold thread and small bead balls. Glue a paper frill or tinsel around the mask.

Materials

thin elastic

silver paper

silver stars

paper plate

thin black card

Batty

A super mask for Hallowe'en.

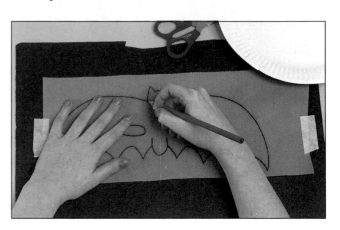

1 Trace off the bat template on page 249 on to the black card. Cut out.

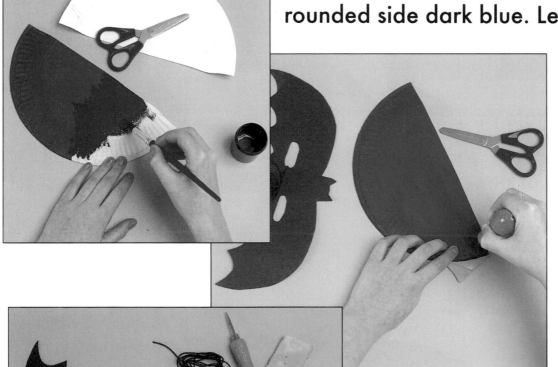

2 Cut the plate in half and paint the rounded side dark blue. Leave to dry.

3 Make a hole on either side of the plate and thread through the elastic (see page 149, step 6).

4 Glue the bat on to the painted side of the plate so that the eye holes come just below the cut edge. Leave the wing tips unglued so that the bat looks as if it is flying.

5 Cut a crescent moon from silver paper.

6 Stick the moon and the silver stars on to the blue plate above the bat.

Adapt the look to become a living spider's web.

Butterfly Wings

A beautiful butterfly mask that is sure to get you noticed.

Materials

2 pipe cleaners

sticky shapes

coloured paper

thin elastic

1 Trace off the template on page 248 on to a piece of folded coloured paper. Cut out. Open the paper to reveal the butterfly.

2 Tear strips and circles from coloured paper.

3 Stick the torn paper on to the front of the mask to decorate it. As you build up the pattern make sure that it is the same on both sides of the fold line.

4 Trim the ends of the paper strips to the shape of the butterfly wings.

5 To finish decorating the mask add sticky shapes to it.

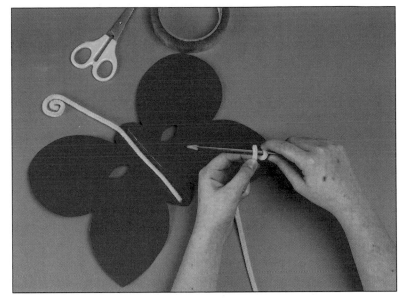

6 Curl one end of the pipe cleaners around a pencil. Tape the uncurled ends to the back of the butterfly.

To fit the elastic to the finished mask, follow the instructions on page 149 (step 6).

Fantastic Fox

A full face mask that will fox your friends! How long will it take them to guess who is beneath those whiskers?

1 Trace off the template on page 250 on to card and cut out. Carefully cut along the marked lines.

2 Overlap the card at each slit and tape together to make a shallow bowl shape.

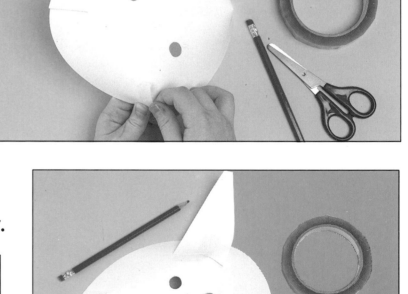

3 Use the template on page 250 to cut 2 ears from card. Cut along the marked lines, overlap and tape together.

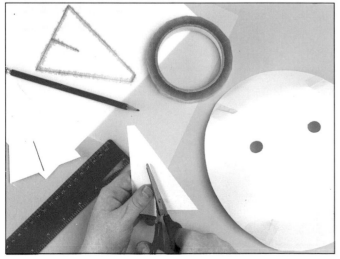

4 Tape the ears to the top of the front of the mask.

5 To make a nose, tape the cup on to the mask below the eye holes.

6 Decorate the top half of the mask with brown paint. Leave to dry then paint the tip of the nose black.

7 Make 3 small holes on either side of the cup nose with the point of a pencil. Cut the pipe cleaners in half and push through the holes for whiskers.

To fit the elastic to the finished mask, follow the instructions on page 149 (step 6).

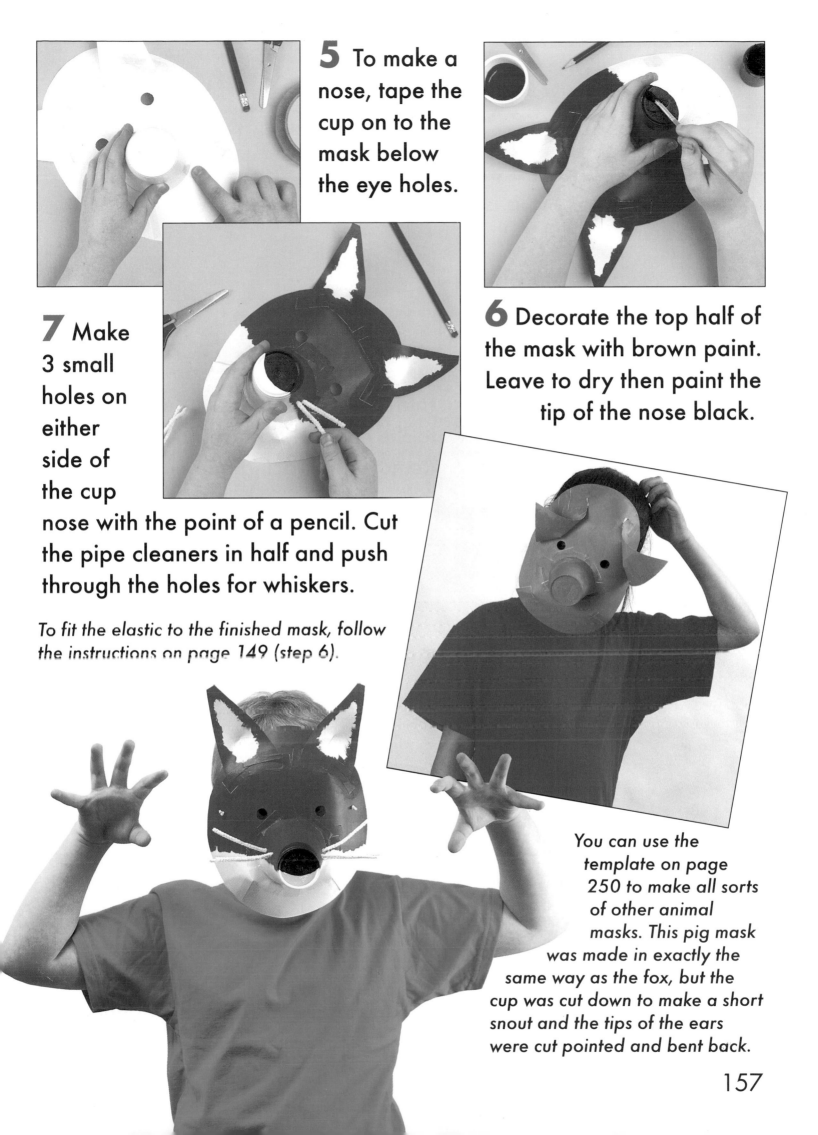

You can use the template on page 250 to make all sorts of other animal masks. This pig mask was made in exactly the same way as the fox, but the cup was cut down to make a short snout and the tips of the ears were cut pointed and bent back.

Bug Eyed

If you've ever wondered what a fly's world looks like, this is your chance to find out.

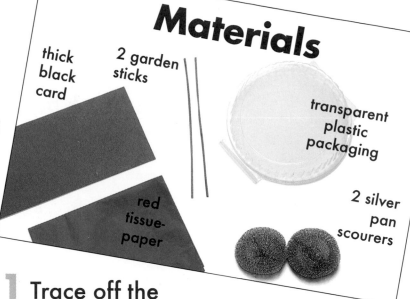

Materials

thick black card

2 garden sticks

transparent plastic packaging

red tissue-paper

2 silver pan scourers

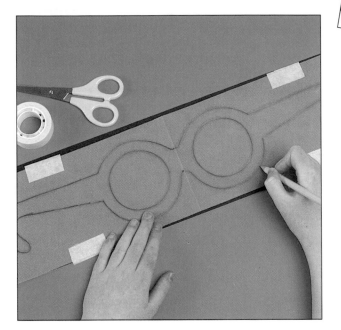

1 Trace off the template on page 251 on to a piece of folded tracing paper. Tape the tracing to the card and go over the outline. Remove the tracing and cut out.

! 2 To make hinged arms for the glasses, ask an adult to use a metal ruler and a craft knife to score a line on either side of the frames. Bend the card carefully along each scored line.

3 Glue the pan scourers to the front of the frames and press down firmly. Leave to dry.

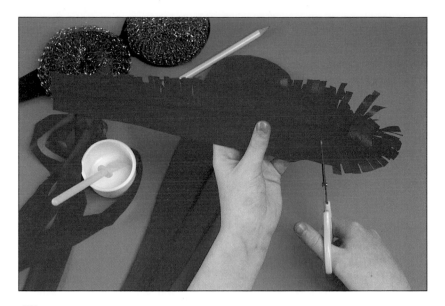

4 Glue a garden stick between 2 strips of tissue-paper and leave to dry. Trim the edge of the paper close to the stick at the bottom, widening out towards the top. Cut into a curve at the top. Make 2.

5 Fringe the paper all the way around the edges. Tape the antennae to the back of the glasses.

The finished insect glasses.

6 Lay a piece of transparent plastic over an eye hole and roughly mark on the shape. Cut out a circle of plastic slightly larger than the marked shape and tape to the back of the mask. Cover the other eye hole in the same way.

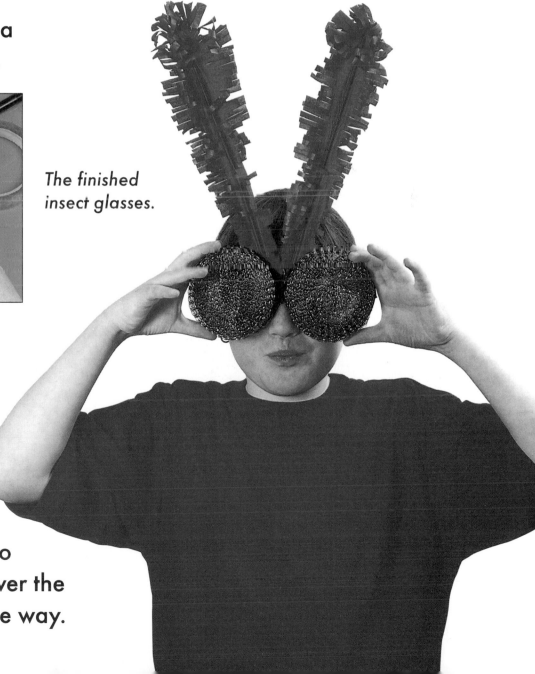

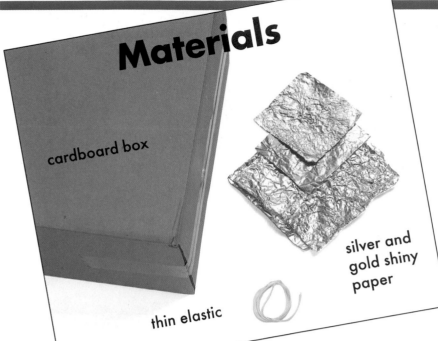

Materials

cardboard box

silver and gold shiny paper

thin elastic

Happy and Sad

How are you feeling today? This mask will keep everyone guessing.

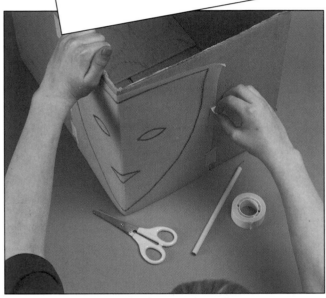

⚠ 1 Trace off the template on page 251 on to folded tracing paper. Tape the tracing on to the box with the fold line laying on a corner edge. Go over the outline of the mask to mark it on to the box. Remove the tracing paper. Ask an adult to cut out the mask for you using a craft knife.

2 Paint one half of the mask red and leave to dry. Then paint the other half blue.

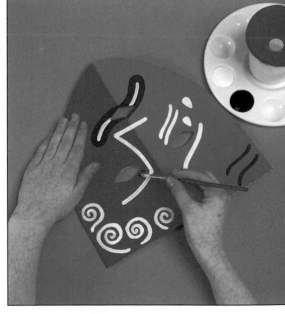

3 Paint a face on to the mask. Show a happy, upward-curving mouth on the red side and a sad, down-turned mouth on the blue side.

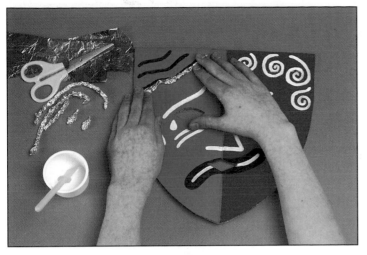

4 Twist together silver paper strips and glue to the blue side to make strands of wavy hair. Scrunch up 2 balls of silver paper to make teardrops and glue to the cheek.

5 Glue curls of twisted gold paper strips to the red side of the mask for hair. Cut a gold paper circle and glue to the cheek.

There are lots more 'contrast' masks that you could make. This one shows the night on one side and the day on the other. Why not make one of your own to show the difference between winter and summer?

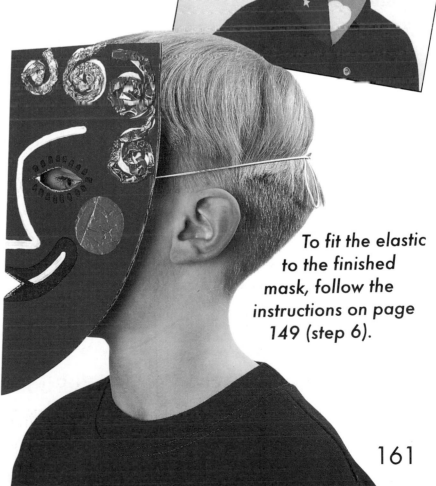

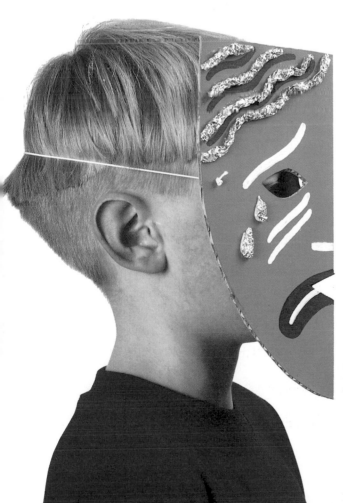

To fit the elastic to the finished mask, follow the instructions on page 149 (step 6).

Clown

One mask that is sure to make them laugh!

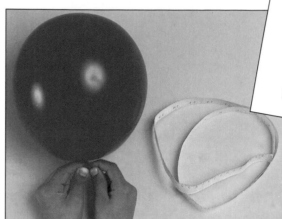

Materials

multi-coloured plastic bags

flour and water paste (see page 256)

newspaper

balloon

! 1 Measure around your head just above your ears. Blow up the balloon until it measures the same size as your head. Tie the end of the balloon in a knot.

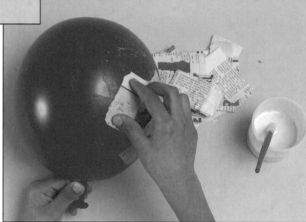

2 Brush the balloon with paste and cover with small strips of newspaper. Add another 3 or 4 layers. Leave to dry out in a warm place for at least 24 hours.

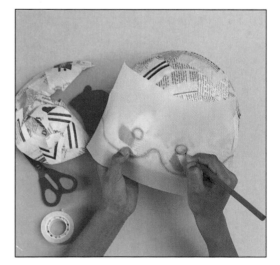

3 Cut off the bottom third of the balloon. Use template B on page 248 to trace off the eye holes and the bottom outline of the mask.

4 Continue the line around the sides of the balloon, curving up over your ears. Cut out.

5 Paint the outside of the balloon white and leave to dry. Now mark on eyelashes and high curved eyebrows.

6 To make the hair, cut the plastic bags into long strips. Fold the strips in half, gather the folded ends together and glue along the inside edge of the mask.

TIP BOX
If you find that the papier mâché balloon is a snug fit, you can glue the hair to the outside edge instead.

Why not make a complete clown of yourself? Use face paints to cover the lower half of your face. Pin a ribbon bow tie to your T-shirt and wear a small party hat on top of the mask.

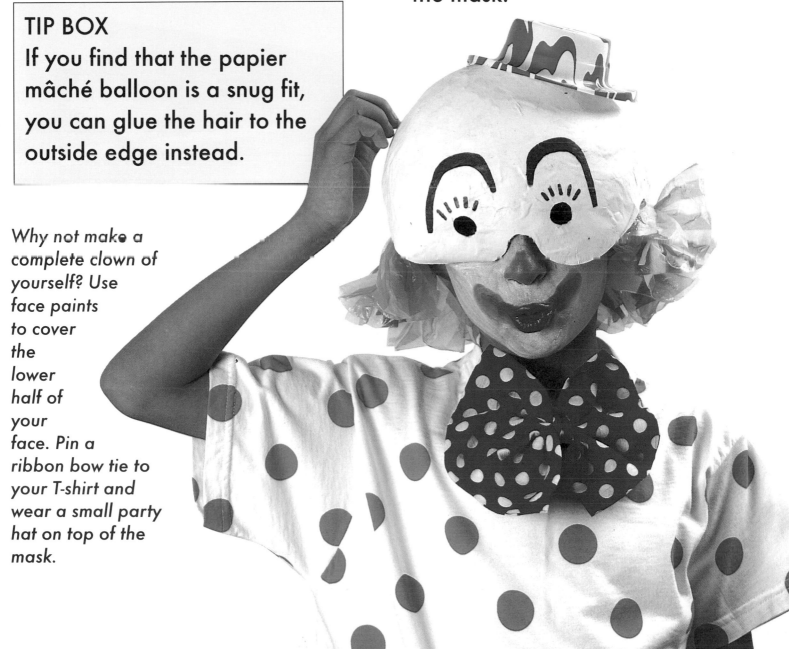

Paint

What you will need

Before you begin the projects in this chapter, it is a good idea to collect together some useful tools first. You will need scissors for cutting; a pencil, eraser and ruler for drawing and marking out; and glue for fixing things together. You will need paper to paint onto, and, of course, paint. Turn the page for advice on paint-brushes, as well as some other ideas for putting paint on paper.

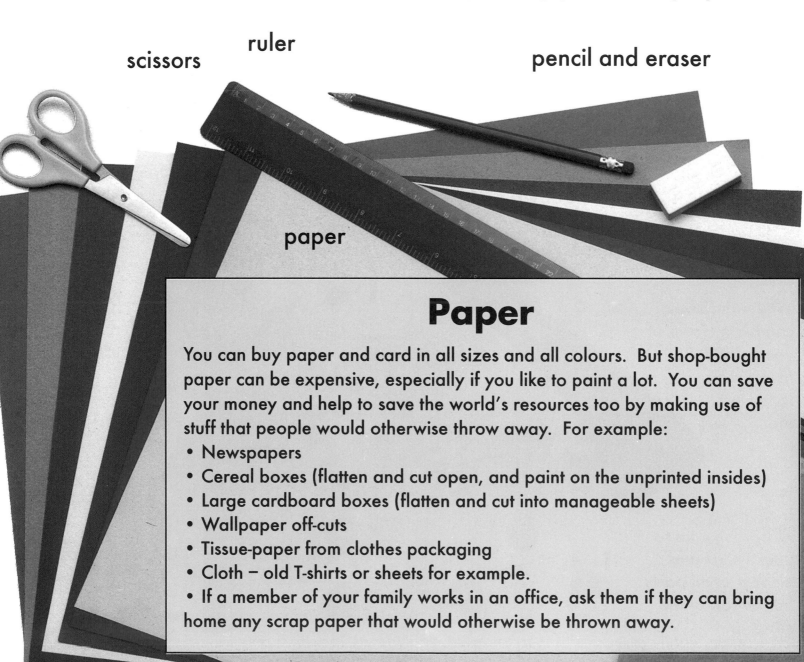

scissors

ruler

pencil and eraser

paper

Paper

You can buy paper and card in all sizes and all colours. But shop-bought paper can be expensive, especially if you like to paint a lot. You can save your money and help to save the world's resources too by making use of stuff that people would otherwise throw away. For example:
• Newspapers
• Cereal boxes (flatten and cut open, and paint on the unprinted insides)
• Large cardboard boxes (flatten and cut into manageable sheets)
• Wallpaper off-cuts
• Tissue-paper from clothes packaging
• Cloth – old T-shirts or sheets for example.
• If a member of your family works in an office, ask them if they can bring home any scrap paper that would otherwise be thrown away.

Paint

Water-based paints have been used for all the projects in this chapter. You can buy them ready-mixed in large, easy-to-use, squeezy bottles. The basic colours you will need are red, yellow, blue, black and white. From these you can mix all other colours, as you will see on page 168. You can use acrylic paints which come in tubes, but do avoid powder paints: they are dusty, difficult to make up and the colours do not mix well.

Add water to paint to make it thinner or PVA glue to make it thicker.

metal ruler

card

string

craft knife

masking tape

PVA glue

felt-tip pens

water-based paint

acrylic paint

wax crayons

oil-based crayons

tissue-paper

Remember

☆ Wear an apron and cover the work area.
☆ Always ask an adult for help when you see this sign [!]
☆ Clear up after yourself.

Brush Up On Painting

When you begin to paint, you will need to paint with something. The first thing you might think of is a paint brush, but there are lots of other things you could use. Blow puddles of thin paint around with a straw. Use your fingers, hands or cut vegetables to print with. Make a card comb and twist it through thick paint, or dabble and smear paint on with a rag. Draw with a twig dipped in thin paint. Last but not least, look at all the different kinds of brushes you could use and try them out for yourself.

plastic comb

plastic straws

twig

card comb

cut potato

roller

hands

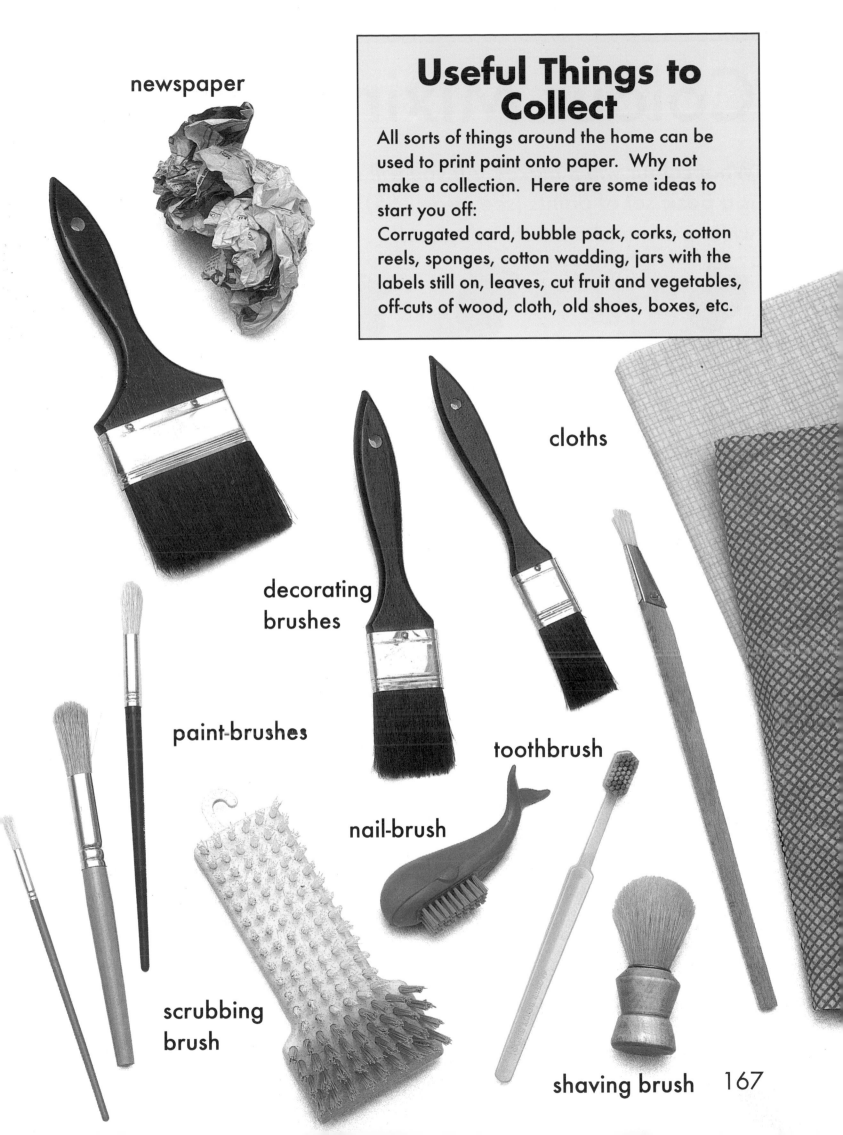

newspaper

Useful Things to Collect

All sorts of things around the home can be used to print paint onto paper. Why not make a collection. Here are some ideas to start you off:

Corrugated card, bubble pack, corks, cotton reels, sponges, cotton wadding, jars with the labels still on, leaves, cut fruit and vegetables, off-cuts of wood, cloth, old shoes, boxes, etc.

cloths

decorating brushes

paint-brushes

toothbrush

nail-brush

scrubbing brush

shaving brush

167

Colour Mixing

What colour will it make? All you will need is a basic set of paints (see page 165), a white plate and a brush to find out!

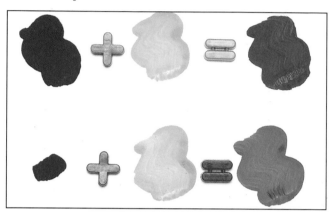

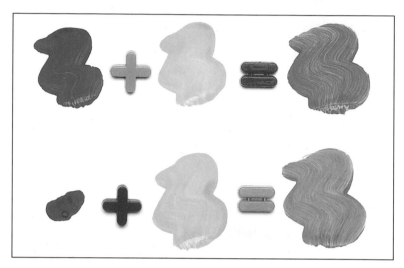

Mix red and yellow to make orange. Add more red for a warmer orange and more yellow for a tangerine shade.

Blue and yellow mixed together makes green. You can vary the shade by adding more or less yellow or blue.

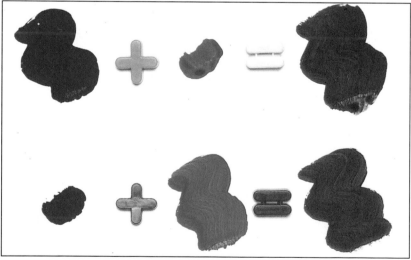

Mix a brushful of red with a drop of blue. Now try a drop of red with a brushful of blue. How is it different?

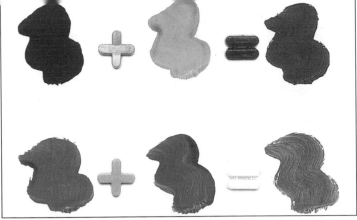

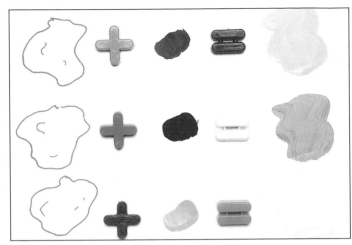

Red and green mixed together makes brown. Now try orange and blue.

To make pastel colours, simply add a drop of any coloured paint to white paint.

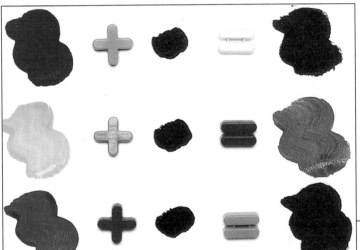

Now see what happens when you mix a drop of black to any colour.

Skin tones are harder to mix. Here are a couple of examples. Now try to mix a colour to match your skin.

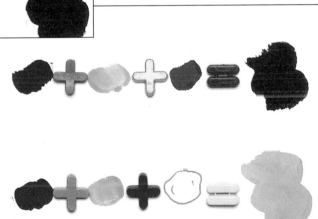

Squeeze small amounts of paint onto an old saucer or plate, or even a thick piece of card. Use a brush to mix them together.

What an Effect

Have a go at using some of the tools on pages 166 and 167 to explore these painting techniques.

Stippling

Cut out a shape from paper and place onto a sheet of card. Dab around the edges of the cut-out shape with a lightly-painted brush.

Dry Brush

Put a little paint onto the tip of a dry brush and work it into the bristles by brushing lightly on newspaper. Now paint onto paper – try adding other colours.

Rolling and combing

1 Roll a thick layer of paint onto a sheet of card. If you do not have a roller, use a jar with the label still on it.

2 Make a comb by cutting teeth along one edge of a square of thick card. Drag and twist the comb through the paint.

Splattering

Dip a toothbrush into some watered-down paint. Run a paint-brush handle along its bristles to splatter the paint onto the paper. What effect will you get with a nail-brush?

Newspaper Crumple

Screw a piece of newspaper into a crumpled ball. Dab into paint and print onto paper. Use other balls of crumpled paper to add more colours.

IN THE FRAME

Frame your pictures as you paint them. Cut two L-shaped pieces of thick card. Position these onto the paper so that they mark off a rectangular area. Paint within this area and then remove the card pieces for an instant frame.

You can use all sorts of things collected from around the house to paint with. Now see what you can find.

The Background Story

Why use only plain paper to draw or paint on when you can create an interesting textured background?

Streaking and dripping

Dip a middle-sized decorating brush into watered-down paint and hold the brush at the top of the paper. Lift the paper and let the paint drip down.

Washes

Dip a large decorating brush into watered-down paint and brush across the paper. Now add different coloured washes, letting the colours run into each other.

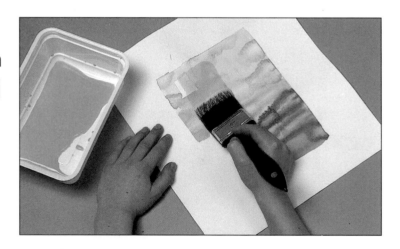

Tonking

1 Paint thickly onto a sheet of paper. Cover an area of the painted paper with newspaper and flatten with your hand.

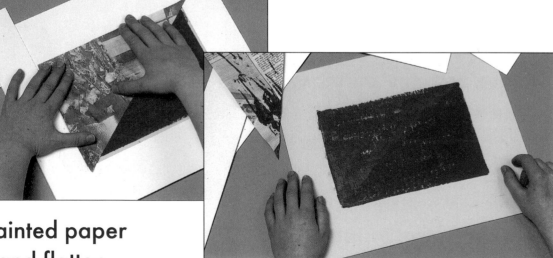

2 Carefully lift off the newspaper.

Rag Rolling

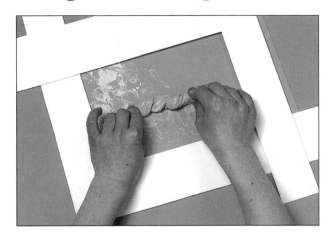

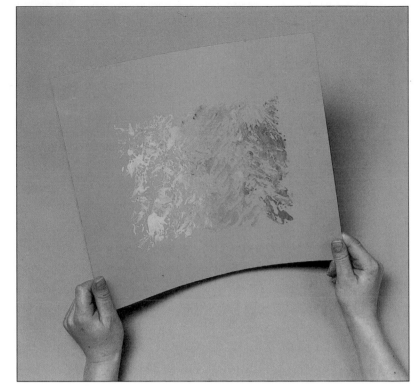

1 Put a rag into a tray of paint and stir until it is well covered. Gather into a wrinkled sausage. Place at the bottom left-hand corner of the paper and roll up.

2 Continue to roll the rag in columns across the paper. If the rag print becomes faint, dip the rag in paint again.

Staining

!1 You can use all sorts of household products to stain white paper, for example shoe polish, turmeric, vinegar, coffee, food colouring and soya sauce. Make up a sample sheet like the one in the photograph.

2 Choose your favourite one and stain some sheets of white paper for future paintings. This tea wash is used as a background for the next project in this book.

Me! Me! Me!

A good place to start painting is with a portrait of yourself.

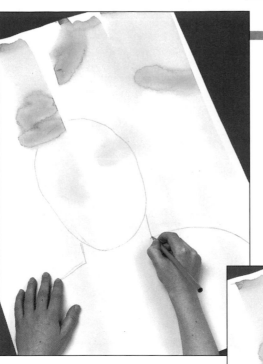

1 Take a textured sheet of paper. Sit in front of a mirror and look at the shape of your face. Draw the outline of it in the centre of the paper.

2 Divide the face up into quarters by marking in light pencil lines horizontally and vertically.

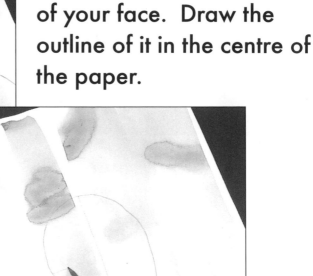

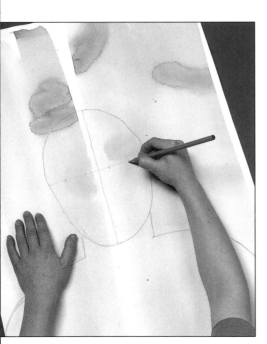

3 Divide the horizontal or eyeline into fifths, to give you a guide for positioning the corners of the eyes.

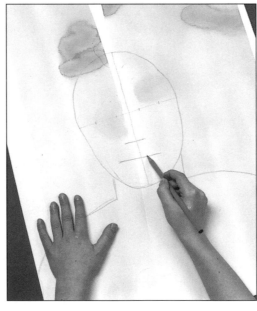

4 Mark in lines for the nose and mouth on the bottom half of the vertical line.

5 Look at your face again. Use the pencil guidelines to help you draw what you see. Rub out these lines when you are happy with your drawing.

174

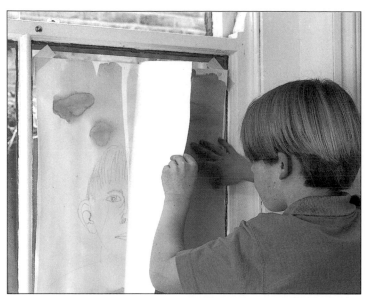

6 Before beginning to paint over your drawing make a copy of it. Tape it onto a window and place a sheet of paper on top of it. Trace off your drawing.

7 Paint over your original drawing. Try to match the colour of your eyes and hair. Mark in any freckles. Don't forget your eyebrows and eyelashes.

Trace copies from your original to make countless versions of yourself.

Fruit and Vegetable Printing

Instead of painting a still life of a bowl of fruit, use the fruit (and some vegetables too) to paint the picture!

⚠ **1** Ask your mum or dad if you can have a selection of fruit and vegetables to paint with.

⚠ **2** Now ask your parent if he or she could cut up the fruit and vegetables so that you can print with them.

3 Put out the colours you will need onto a plate. Paint the cut end of a vegetable and begin to print a border around a large sheet of paper.

4 The painted edge of a carrot stick has been used to print this bowl and the table mat beneath it.

176

5 An apple cut in half and painted has been used to print different coloured apples in the bowl.

6 The round end of a carrot has been used to build up a bunch of grapes. A half a lemon has been used to print an orange. The round end of a carrot painted red makes the cherries.

You can have great fun experimenting with the variety of effects that can be achieved with this simple printing technique.

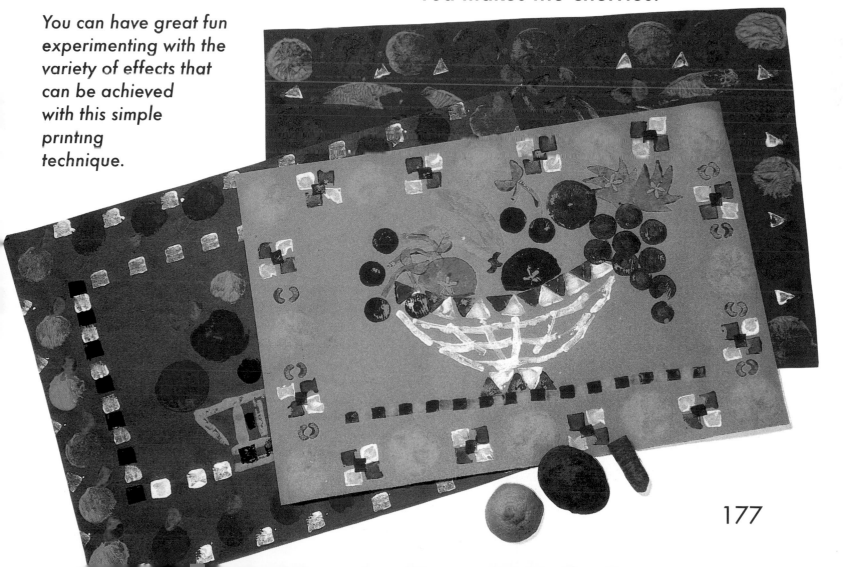

Draw With Glue

A *picture drawn with glue makes a wonderful printing block.*

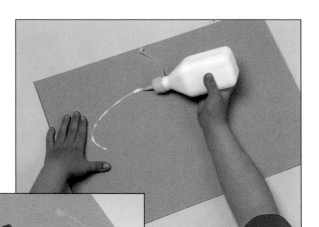

1 Use glue to draw a picture onto a piece of thick card. Leave to dry overnight.

2 When the glue has dried completely, colour in the areas between the lines with wax or oil-based crayons.

3 Paint all over the surface of the card. Work fast so that the paint does not dry.

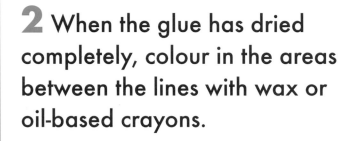

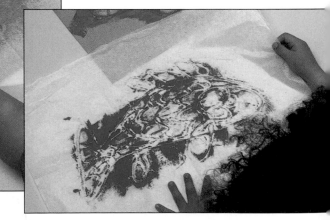

4 Lay a sheet of white tissue-paper over the painted card and smooth down with your hands. Carefully peel back the tissue-paper.

5 Put the tissue-paper print to one side to dry.

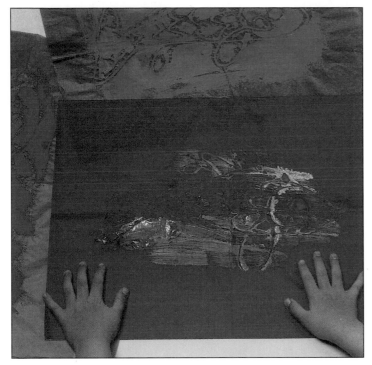

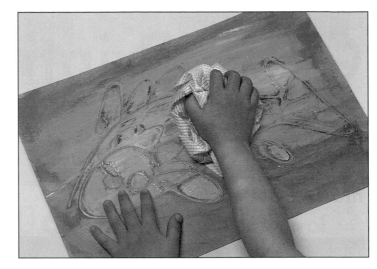

6 Paint all over the card again. This time make a print onto a coloured sheet of tissue-paper. You can make as many prints of your picture as you like.

7 When you have made all the prints you want, use a damp cloth to wipe most of the paint off the card. Leave some paint in the corners. When you have finished, the colour of the crayons should be showing through brightly again.

The printing card has become a picture in itself. Make a frame for it and hang it on the wall.

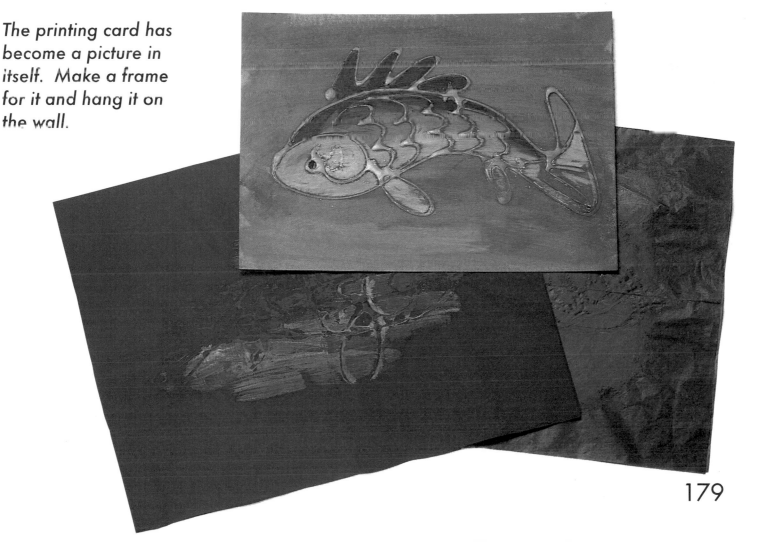

String Pictures

In this project you will use string to draw with, print with and to make a decorative frame.

Materials

shells

string

thick card

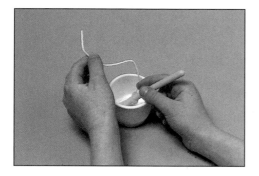

1 Put a long piece of string into a cupful of glue and stir it around.

2 Take the string out of the glue and pull it through your fingers so that it does not drip everywhere.

3 Lay the string on top of a small square of card (12 cm x 12 cm) to make a picture. You may need to cut the string into small pieces. Leave your string picture to dry overnight.

4 Lay paper onto a bed of newspaper. Paint over the string picture and press down hard onto the paper. Make several prints.

182

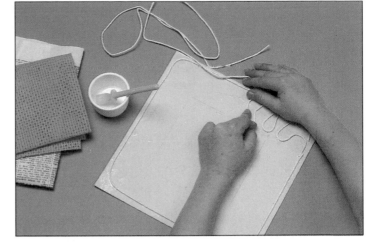

5 Choose your favourite print and frame it. Put the string picture in the centre of a large square of card (17 cm x 17 cm), draw around it and lift it off.

6 Decorate the border by drawing on a pattern with glue-covered string. Stick on some shells. Leave overnight to dry.

7 Colour in the spaces around the string and the shells with wax or oil-based crayons.

8 To give the frame an antique effect, paint all over the card with brown paint. Use a rag to dab off some of the paint.

Cut a print down to fit into the centre of the frame. Glue into place. Ask an adult to hang it up for you.

183

Painter's Sketchbook

Make this book to keep your favourite pictures in.

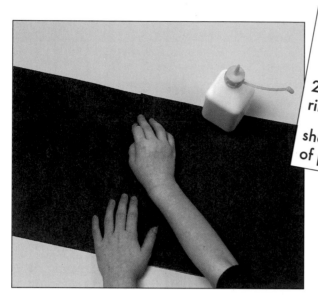

Materials

thick card

cut-out letters

2 ribbons

sheets of paper

2 squares printed cloth

1 Make a long strip of paper by gluing several sheets of paper end to end.

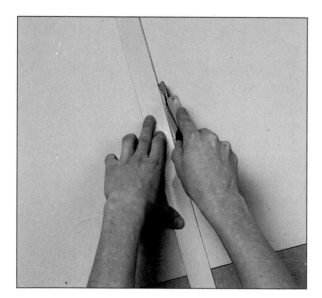

2 Fold evenly into a zig zag.

4 Now cover both pieces of card with the printed cloth made on page 180.

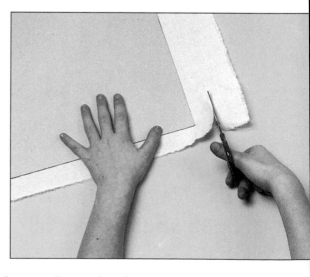

! **3** Cut 2 pieces of thick card about 1 cm larger all around than the folded zig zag of paper.

Place the card on the cloth. Cut around the fabric leaving a 2.5 cm edge.

5 Use a brush to dampen the edges of the cloth with water.

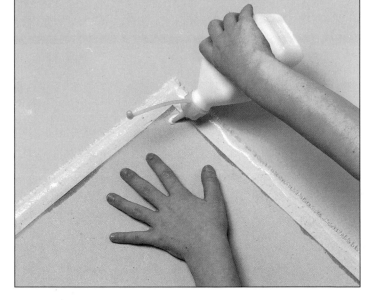

6 Run a line of glue all around the edge of the cloth and a blob on each corner of the card.

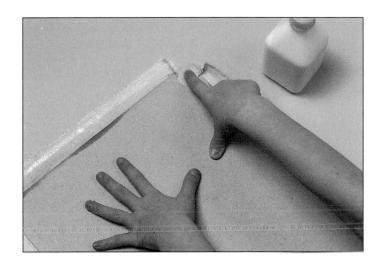

7 Fold the corners of the cloth over onto the card as shown.

8 Fold over the sides of the cloth as shown. Make sure that the corner seams do not overlap each other, and check that the fabric is pulled tight across the front of the card.

9 Glue a length of ribbon onto each piece of card.

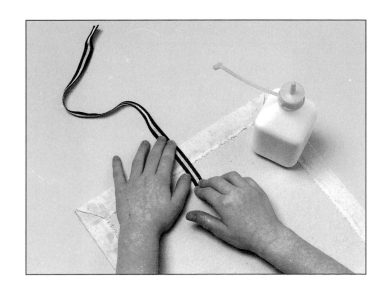

Continues on next page

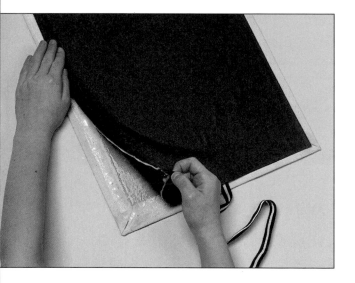

10 Evenly spread a thin layer of glue over both pieces of card.

11 Run a thin line of glue close to the edge of the first page of the zig zag strip of paper. Press the paper onto a piece of covered card.

12 Glue around the last page of the zig zag strip and press onto the second piece of covered card. Make sure that the ribbons are both on the same side so they can be tied together.

14 Cut out letters from magazine or newspaper headlines and make a title for your book.

13 Once the glue has dried (leave overnight) open up the concertina book and print a border around each page using a cut potato.

Fill your book with your favourite pictures painted by you, your family and your friends. When it is full, make a present of it to a friend.

Fresco

Paint a picture onto the plaster surface of a small sheet of plasterboard and hang it on the wall. Plasterboard is cheap and can be bought from any DIY shop.

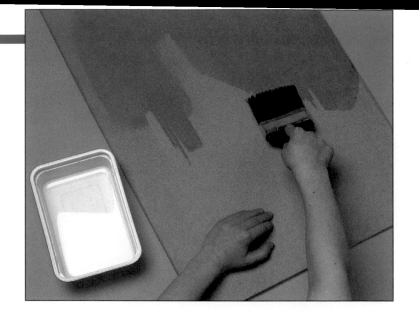

1 Use a large decorating brush to cover both sides of the plasterboard with water. Leave overnight to dry.

2 Mark out a large rectangle on the front of the board leaving an even frame all around.

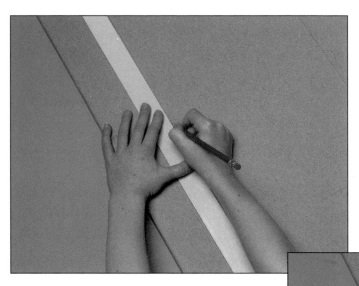

! 3 Ask an adult to cut through the paper along the marked lines just into the plaster below.

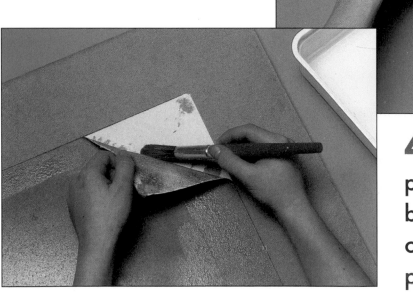

4 Carefully peel back the paper to reveal the plaster below. If the paper does not come away cleanly, run a wet paint-brush under the edge.

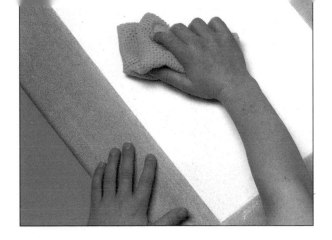

5 Scrub the plaster with a damp cloth. Scrap off any remaining patches of paper with a round-ended knife. Don't worry if the surface of the plaster looks scratched or pitted. This will give a more interesting effect when painted over.

6 Paint a picture onto the plaster using watered-down paint. Try a portrait of your mum or dad, or your pet.

7 Use stencils cut from thin card to decorate the paper frame. Use a thick brush to stipple the paint onto the stencil, taking care not to let paint creep under the edge.

Furniture Painting

An old piece of furniture can be transformed by your imagination and just a little paint. But do ask mum or dad for permission first.

1 Use fine sandpaper to rub down the area of wood to be painted.

2 Put a little washing-up liquid into a bowl of warm water and wash down the sanded wood. Leave to dry.

3 Sketch out a rough design for the area to be painted. This is just a guide, and you can change it as you work.

4 Cut all the stencils you will need from thin card.

5 Work outwards from the centre of your design. Tape the stencil to the wood.

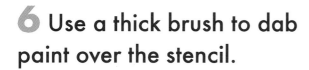

6 Use a thick brush to dab paint over the stencil.

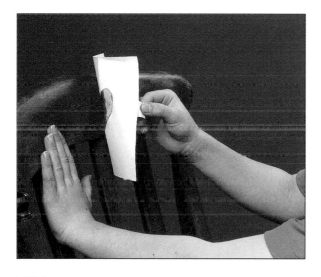

! **7** Carefully peel off the stencil. Build up your design using one stencil at a time. Once the paint has dried ask an adult to help you brush the painted area with a thin coat of varnish

The finished chair. Now everyone will want to sit on it

191

Presents

What you will need

Before you begin to make your presents it is a good idea to get ready a few useful tools. You will need a pencil, eraser and ruler for drawing and marking out; and paint or felt-tip pens for decorating. You can use a pair of round-ended scissors for cutting paper and thin card, but you will need to ask a grown up to cut thick card for you with a craft knife. You can use glue, staplers or tape for fixing things together, and you will need a needle and thread ready for sewing.

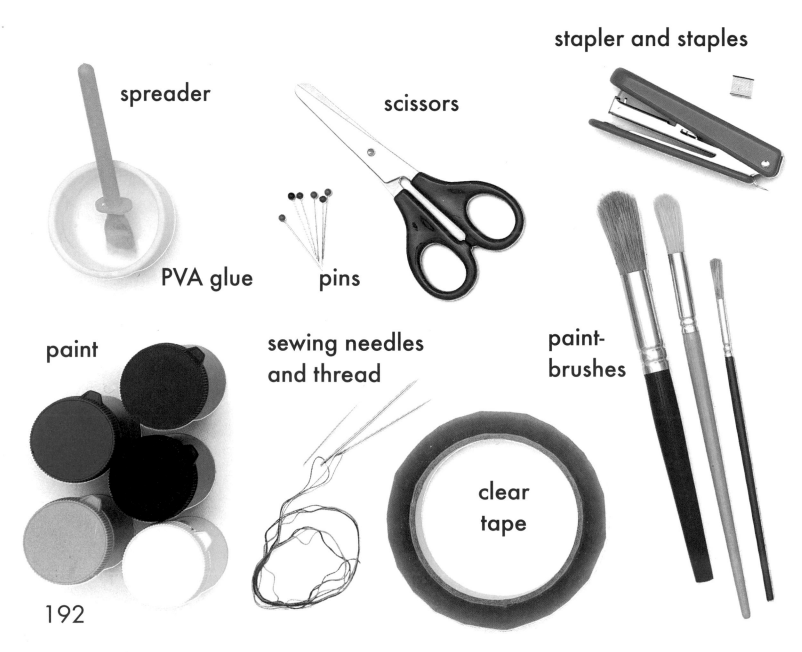

spreader

scissors

stapler and staples

PVA glue

pins

paint

sewing needles and thread

paint-brushes

clear tape

Other Useful Things

When you begin to make presents you will find that all sorts of things come in useful. Listed below are just a few. Collect useful odds and ends in a cardboard box and keep adding to your collection.

Cardboard tubes, yoghurt pots, bottle tops, jar lids, cereal packets, matchboxes, thick card, paper plates, sweet wrappers, tissue-paper, wrapping paper, colour magazines, felt, string, wool oddments, ribbon ends, lolly sticks, material off-cuts, cotton reels, corks, tinsel, pipe cleaners, sequins, glitter, straws, self-adhesive shapes, fir-cones, dried flowers, buttons and beads.

masking tape

tracing paper

thick card

craft knife

felt-tip pens

pencil sharpener

metal ruler

pencil and eraser

plastic ruler

Remember

☆ Wear an apron and cover the work area.
☆ Collect together the items in the materials box at the beginning of each project.
☆ Always ask an adult for help when you see this sign !
☆ Clear up after yourself.

Teddy Bear Pencil Holder

This jolly bear can be hung up on the wall or pinned onto a noticeboard.

Materials

felt

card

ribbon

1 Trace off the teddy bear templates on pages 252 and 253 onto a piece of card and cut out.

2 Use felt-tip pens to colour in the bear's eyes, nose and mouth. Staple the head to the body.

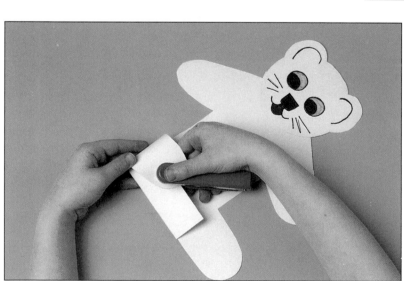

3 Fold up the flap of card at the bottom of the body. Fold the legs inwards over the flap. Staple each leg to the flap to make a pocket.

4 Fold the bear's arms inwards and staple together.

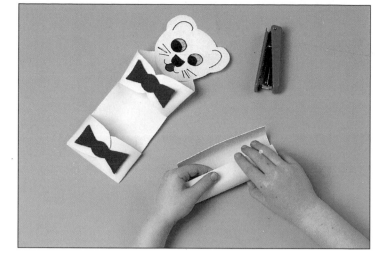

5 Cut 2 bows from the felt and glue over the staples.

6 Cut a piece of card 12 cm x 16 cm, roll up into a tube and staple in place.

7 Tape a ribbon loop to the back of the bear's head to hang it up with. Push the tube down between the paws.

To finish the present off slip some coloured pencils or felt-tip pens into the tube. For Hallowe'en make a black cat holder. For Easter make a rabbit holder and fill it with chocolate eggs.

Butterfly Card

An unusual card that is a present too.

Materials

ribbon — safety pin — sticky pad — thin card — sequins — foil tape — glitter — wrapping paper

1 Cut a piece of card 30 cm x 12 cm. Fold in half.

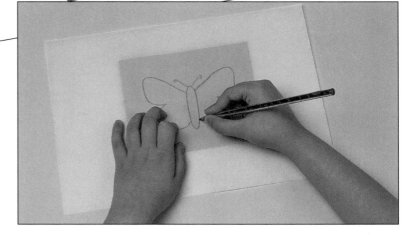

2 Trace off the butterfly template (page 252) onto the front of the card.

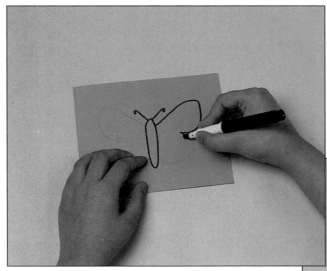

3 Draw round the outline of the butterfly with a black felt-tip pen. Decorate the body.

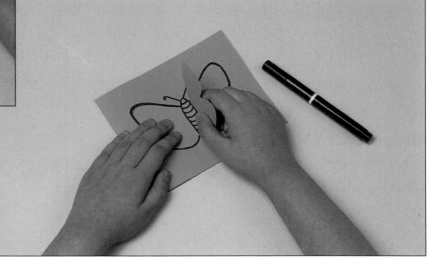

⚠ 4 Cut around the outside of the butterfly wings and lift up.

5 Cut a piece of card 13 cm x 10 cm. Cover both sides with wrapping paper.

6 Open up the card. Tape the covered piece of card in place behind the lifted butterfly.

7 Trace off the butterfly template onto a piece of card and cut out. Decorate the wings with sequins and glitter.

To finish off the card, lay a thin piece of ribbon along the folded edge and tie into a decorative bow on the outside.

8 Tape a small safety pin to the back of the butterfly and secure inside the card with a sticky pad.

Scented Clown

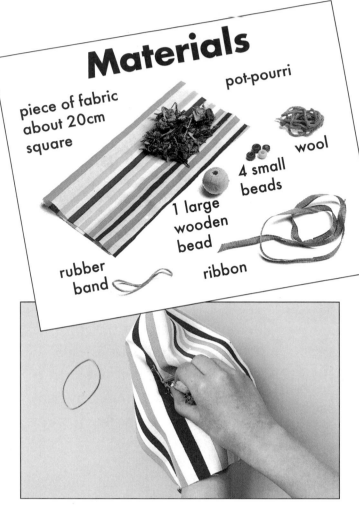

Materials

piece of fabric about 20cm square

pot-pourri

wool

4 small beads

1 large wooden bead

ribbon

rubber band

A colourful clown perfect for hanging in the wardrobe to keep clothes smelling sweet.

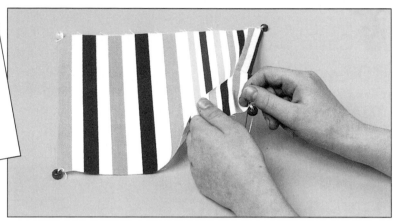

1 Sew a bead onto each corner of the piece of fabric.

2 Put a heap of pot-pourri in the middle of the fabric. Gather up the edges to make a ball and fasten securely with the rubber band.

3 Paint the large wooden bead white. When it is dry, draw on a clown's face with felt-tip pens.

4 Cut 12 pieces of wool each measuring about 5 cm. Tie into a bundle and secure with a knot.

The finished clown can be hung on a coat hanger.

5 Thread wool onto a needle and sew a couple of stitches through the back of the wig.

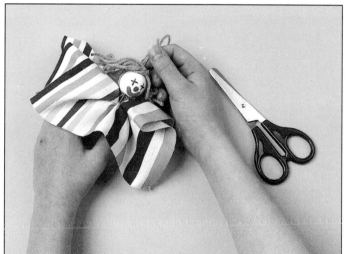

6 Now thread on the clown's head and sew securely onto the bag.

7 Thread a ribbon through the top of the clown's wig and knot the ends together.

199

Ollie Octopus

A perfect present for a friend to hang from the bedroom ceiling.

Materials

chunky wool

newspaper

string

joggle eyes

bits of felt

crêpe paper

elastic

card

1 Roll some newspaper into a ball and tape it into shape.

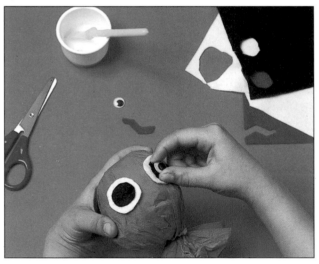

2 Cover the ball with crêpe paper. Tie a piece of string tightly around the neck, leaving a frill.

3 Glue 2 black felt circles onto 2 larger white felt circles and stick onto the ball. Stick the joggle eyes on top. Cut a zig zag mouth from red felt and glue on too.

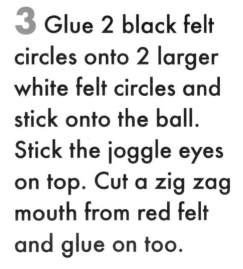

4 Cut 8 pieces of thick wool each 25 cm long. Tape these evenly along a strip of card 15 cm x 3 cm.

200

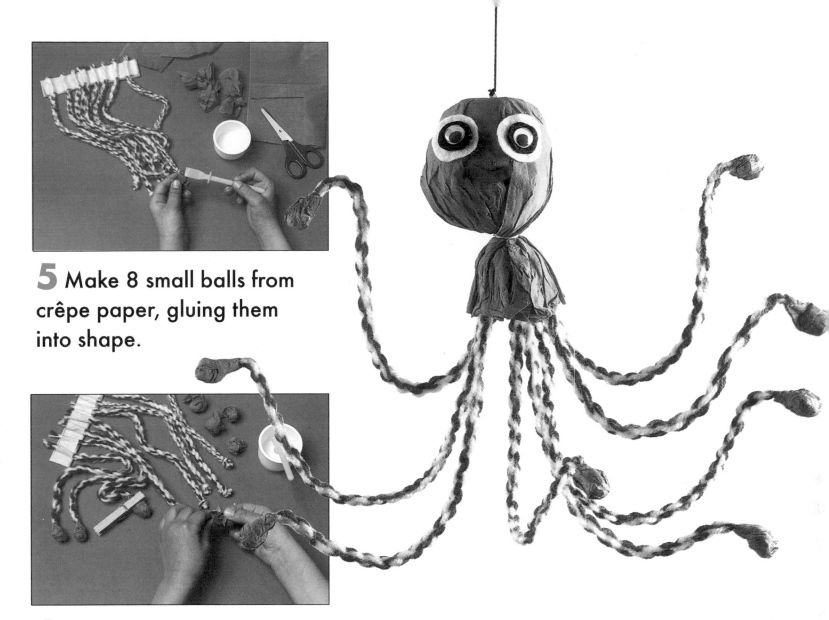

5 Make 8 small balls from crêpe paper, gluing them into shape.

6 Glue a ball to the bottom of each piece of wool.

Fasten a piece of elastic to Ollie's head so that he bounces up and down when he is hung up.

7 Tape the card strip into a circle and glue it inside the frill of the neck.

OTHER IDEAS

For a Hallowe'en gift
Make a spider out of black paper and use pipe cleaners for the legs.
For a gift for a newborn baby
Use pastel colours and securely sew bells to the ends of the wool. Hang above the baby's cot well out of reach.

201

wrapping paper

strips of crêpe paper

washing-up liquid bottle

box

6 garden sticks

coloured card

Ringo

Make this game for a brother or sister, then play it together to see who can get the best score.

1 Choose a wrapping paper with a repeat pattern and cut out 6 figures from it. Glue these onto thin card and cut around the outline.

2 Tape each figure to the top of a garden stick.

3 Cover the box with wrapping paper.

!4 Poke 6 holes through the top of the box, spacing them out evenly.

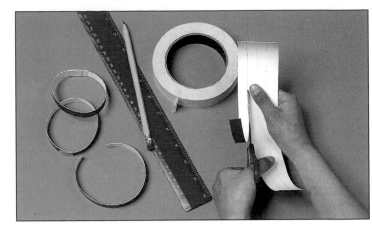

5 Use a coin or small bottle lid to draw out 6 circles from coloured card. Cut out and number them 1 to 6. Glue a number next to each hole.

6 Cut open a washing-up liquid bottle. Cut 6 1-cm strips from the plastic. Tape the strips into rings.

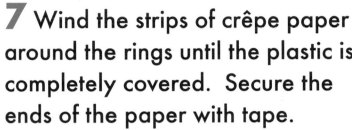

7 Wind the strips of crêpe paper around the rings until the plastic is completely covered. Secure the ends of the paper with tape.

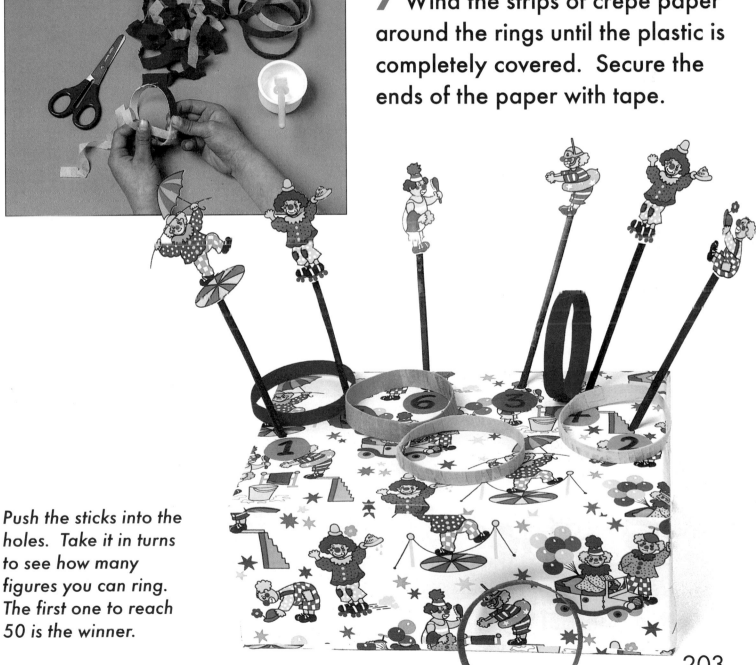

Push the sticks into the holes. Take it in turns to see how many figures you can ring. The first one to reach 50 is the winner.

Wizard Birthday Badge

Make this super badge for a friend to wear on his or her birthday.

Materials

felt · wooden dolly peg · safety pin · self-adhesive stars · cotton wool · thin card

1 Mark in a face on the head of the peg with felt-tip pens.

2 Cut a piece of black felt 15 cm x 9 cm. Sew a line of running stitches up one long edge, leaving about 10 cm of thread at each end.

3 Pull both ends of the thread to gather up the felt. Put the dress around the peg's neck and tie securely at the back.

4 Cut 2 arms from white card and glue onto the dress. Cut a number (the age of your friend) from the gold card and stick onto the front of the dress.

5 Cut a piece of purple felt 8 cm x 8 cm and sew a line of running stitches along one edge. Gather the stitches.

6 Put the cloak over the dress and tie securely at the front of the wizard's neck. Decorate with stars.

7 Cut a circle of blue card and fold into 4. Cut along one fold line to the middle. Put glue along one cut edge and slide under the other to make a cone shape. Decorate with stars.

8 Glue some cotton-wool onto the head for the hair and a beard and stick the hat on top. Attach a safety pin to the back of the cloak.

For Hallowe'en make a peg doll witch and give her a broom to hold.

205

Elephant Memo Clip

The perfect present for a busy parent.

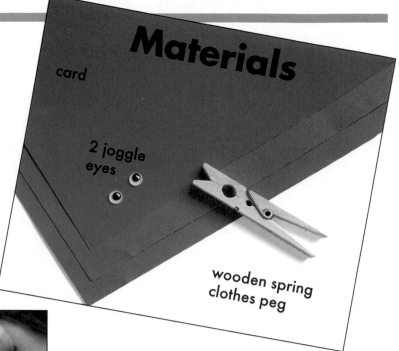

Materials

card

2 joggle eyes

wooden spring clothes peg

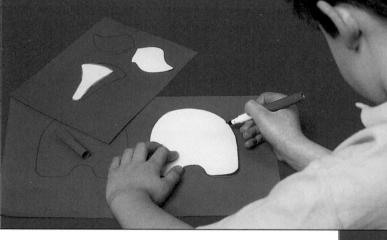

1 Trace off the elephant templates on page 253 onto stiff card. You will need 2 bodies, 2 ears and 1 trunk.

2 Cut out and decorate with paint and felt-tip pens.

3 Glue the peg between the front and back of the elephant's body so that it sticks out at the top by about 1 cm. Leave to dry.

4 Glue the ears behind the front of the body. Leave to dry.

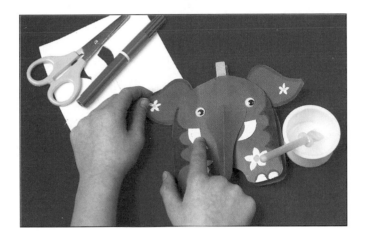

6 Stick on the joggle eyes. Draw and cut out 2 tusks from white card. Glue these on either side of the trunk.

5 Make a fold down the middle of the trunk. Glue onto the centre of the elephant's face.

If you use a bulldog clip instead of a peg, the memo clip can be hung on a pin. You can vary the design too.

Funny Face Kite

Make 2 of these and fly them with a friend.

Materials

coloured tissue-paper

thick card

thin white paper

crêpe paper

string

1 Cut 2 strips of card measuring 26 cm x 2 cm and 17 cm x 2 cm. Staple into a cross. Glue the card cross onto a large piece of crêpe paper and leave to dry.

2 Mark a line across each corner of the paper about 1 cm from the card cross. Cut along these lines. Fold over the edge of paper all the way round and glue down.

3 To strengthen the cross stick pieces of masking tape over it.

4 Cut out and colour 2 eyes, a nose and a mouth. Stick onto the front of the kite.

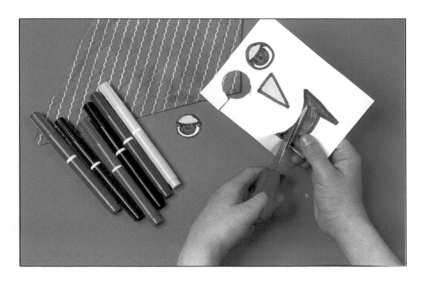

5 Fold a piece of masking tape into a square and cut a hole in the centre of it. Make 3. Tape the squares to the side and bottom corners of the kite.

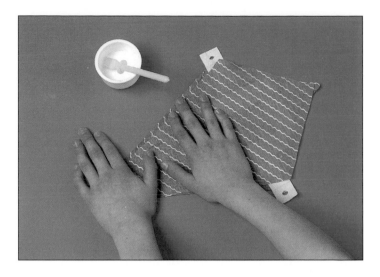

6 Cover the back of the kite with a piece of crêpe paper cut to fit and glued in place.

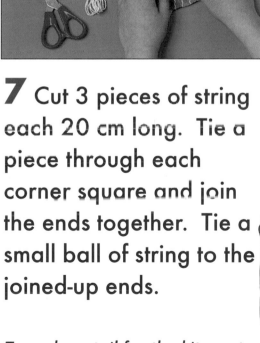

7 Cut 3 pieces of string each 20 cm long. Tie a piece through each corner square and join the ends together. Tie a small ball of string to the joined-up ends.

To make a tail for the kite, cut a piece of string 40 cm long. Tie bits of coloured tissue-paper onto the string and tape it to the bottom of the kite. Thread long strips of coloured tissue-paper through the side holes to make tassels.

209

Photo Frame

Put a picture of yourself in this present and give it to your grandparents.

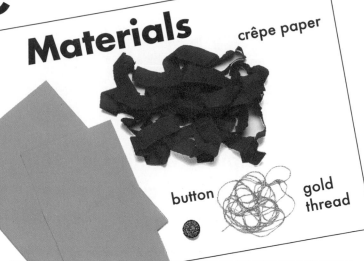

Materials

thick card

crêpe paper

button

gold thread

1 Cut out 2 pieces of card each measuring 20 cm x 16 cm. Draw a line as wide as your ruler all the way round one piece of card. Cut out the middle space.

2 Wind 2-cm wide strips of crêpe paper around the cardboard frame, fixing in place with a dab of glue here and there.

3 Tie the gold thread to the frame and wrap it round and round. Secure the thread with a knot at the back.

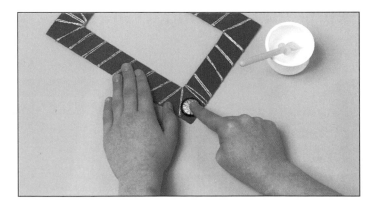

4 Glue a large button to one corner.

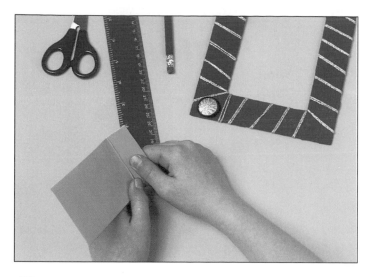

5 Cut out a piece of card measuring 13 cm x 6 cm. Draw a line 2 cm in from the edge. Score along the line and gently bend back.

6 Glue the support arm onto the back card 10 cm up from the bottom edge and secure with masking tape. Leave under a weight to dry.

7 Put glue along 3 sides of the back card leaving the top edge unglued. Press the covered frame onto it and leave under a weight to dry.

When the glue has dried, you can slip a photo of yourself into the frame.

Flower Cart

The perfect present for Mother's Day.

small cardboard box

thin blue card

coloured tissue-paper

thin white card

1 Put the box on a sheet of tissue-paper. Push the paper over the edges of the box and secure with glue.

2 Cut a strip of blue card 18 cm x 2 cm. Decorate with felt-tip pens.

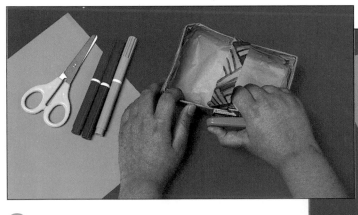

3 Staple the decorated strip of card to the box to make a handle.

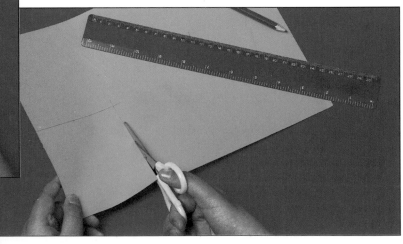

4 To make an awning for the cart, cut a piece of blue card 10 cm x 9 cm. Decorate with stripes.

212

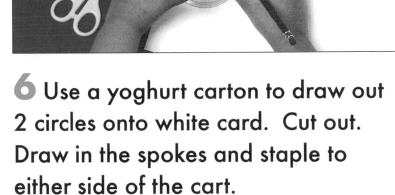

5 Fold the card in half and staple to the handle.

6 Use a yoghurt carton to draw out 2 circles onto white card. Cut out. Draw in the spokes and staple to either side of the cart.

The flower cart, brimming with tissue-paper flowers, will make a beautiful table or windowsill decoration.

7 Crumple up some green tissue-paper and fill the cart with it. Cut out flower shapes from coloured tissue-paper and glue onto the green base. Stick small balls of coloured tissue-paper in the centre of the flower shapes.

Eggs in a Basket

A colourful surprise for Easter Day!

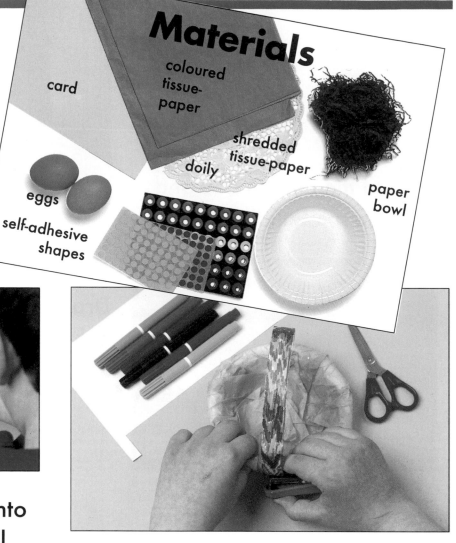

Materials

card

coloured tissue-paper

shredded tissue-paper

doily

paper bowl

eggs

self-adhesive shapes

1 Place the paper bowl onto a piece of tissue-paper. Pull the paper over the edges of the bowl and smooth down.

2 For a handle, cut a strip of card, decorate and staple to the bowl.

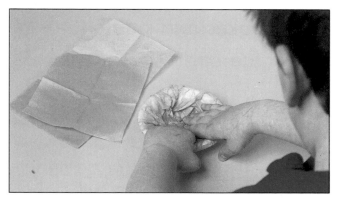

3 Glue a thin strip of blue tissue-paper around the bowl. Stick bits cut from the doily to the rim of the bowl. Fill with shredded tissue-paper.

4 Make a hole at the top of an egg with a darning needle. Make a larger hole at the bottom.

5 Hold the egg over a bowl and blow through the smaller hole until the egg is empty. Carefully rinse and drain the egg.

6 When the egg is dry cover the holes with masking tape. Paint the egg all over.

Place the decorated eggs in the basket on a nest of shredded tissue-paper. Scatter small sugar or chocolate eggs all around. You could make a gift tag from card and tie it on to the handle.

7 When the paint is dry, decorate the egg with self-adhesive shapes.

Mini Felt Stockings

The perfect present for the Christmas tree.

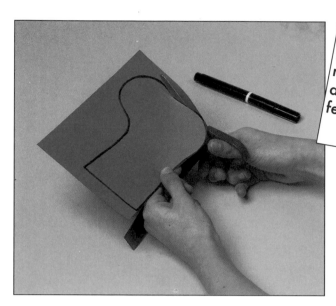

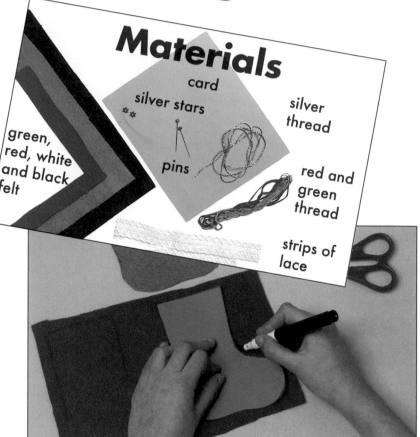

Materials

card

silver stars

silver thread

green, red, white and black felt

pins

red and green thread

strips of lace

1 Trace off the stocking on page 253 onto card and cut out to make a template.

2 Draw round the stocking template twice on the red felt and twice on the green felt. Cut out. Pin the red stockings together and the green stockings together.

3 Sew an even line of running stitches around the stockings, leaving the tops open.

4 Cut 2 small pieces of lace to fit around the top of the stockings. Glue in place.

5 Cut 2 snowmen from white felt (template on page 252) and glue to the stockings. Mark faces and buttons with felt-tip pen.

6 Cut 2 hats from black felt (template page 252) and glue in place. Stick a silver star above the snowmen.

7 Sew a loop of silver thread through the top of each stocking. They can be hung from a tree and filled with small presents.

Make several stockings, one for each member of your family, and decorate each with a different Christmas design.

Fancy Dressing

What you will need

Whether you will be making the projects in this chapter for your dressing up box or to create a special costume for a fancy dress party, you should get together a few tools first. You'll need scissors or pinking shears for cutting (ask a grown up to cut thick card for you with a craft knife); a pair of compasses for making circles; a bradawl and a hole punch to make holes; glue, tape and staples to fix things together; and a needle and thread ready for sewing. Paint, felt-tip pens and fabric crayons will all come in useful for decorating.

needle and thread

clear glue

pliers

PVA glue and spreader

felt-tip pens

plastic tape

paint-brushes

clear tape

masking tape

double-sided tape

glitter glue

paint

Other Useful Things

Dressing Up Box
It is a good idea to start a collection of old clothes for dressing up in. Store them in an old basket or box. Visit jumble sales and second-hand shops. Collect all sorts of hats, scarves, bags, ties, shoes, and jewellery. Keep old pillowcases and sheets (to turn into robes) and towels and curtains (to transform into cloaks).

Face Paints
Face paints are a good way to finish off a fancy dress outfit. Some of the children in this book are wearing face paints. Have a go at trying to copy the way they look.

safety pins

tracing paper

craft knife

thick card

pencil and eraser

metal ruler

pinking shears

scissors

bradawl

stapler and staples

hole punch

pair of compasses

fabric crayons

Remember

☆ Wear an apron and cover the work area.
☆ Collect together the items in the materials box at the beginning of each project.
☆ Always ask an adult for help when you see this sign [!]
☆ Clear up after yourself.

ruler

Clown

A pair of baggy clown's trousers that come with a joke attached. Ask a friend to pull the hankie from your pocket and watch his surprise as it gets longer and longer!

Hoop Trousers

Materials

pyjama trousers

wool

plastic-covered wire

8 material squares

gift ribbon

thick card 20 x 30 cm

safety pin

1 Replace the pyjama cord with plastic-covered wire. Twist the ends together.

2 Knot the squares of material together to make a long string. Pin to the inside of the waistband.

3 To make a 'pocket' cut a 10-cm slit on one side of the pyjamas just beneath the waistband. Pull the string of hankies through the slit.

Wig

4 Wind the wool and then the ribbon around the long edge of the card until it is covered at least twice.

6 Cut through the wool and ribbon along the unsewn edge of the card.

Use a small pair of braces to keep the trousers up. Choose a big, bright T-shirt to wear underneath. Gift bows make perfect 'buttons'.

5 Sew in and out of the strands of wool and ribbon along one side of the card, from one end to the other and back again.

Keep the wig in place with hair grips and cut a fringe at the front.

Borrow Dad's shoes and use ribbons for laces.

Pirate

Before you sail the seven seas in search of treasure, take the time to make this hook and cutlass.

Hook

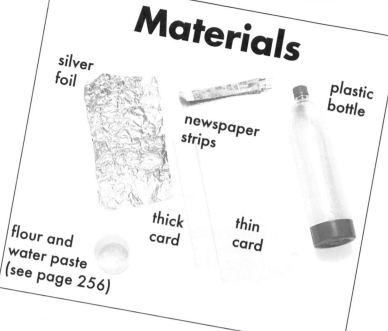

Materials

silver foil

newspaper strips

plastic bottle

thick card

thin card

flour and water paste (see page 256)

[!] **1** Cut the top off the plastic bottle and paint black.

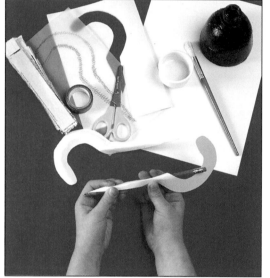

2 Trace the template on page 254 on to a folded piece of thin card. Cut out. Press each card piece around a pencil to begin to make a hook shape.

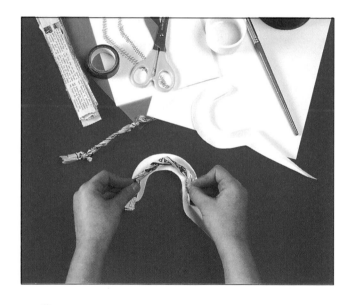

3 Twist some newspaper strips together and sandwich between the 2 pieces of card. Tape in place at the top, middle and bottom.

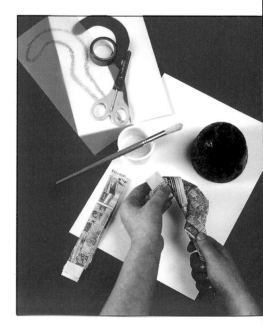

4 Brush the hook with paste and wrap newspaper strips around it. Put on several layers pasting in between.

Tie a scarf around your head and keep in place with an elastic band. A curtain ring makes the perfect earring.

Make this eye patch from black felt or card using the template on page 254 and attach a piece of black elastic to each side.

5 Once the hook has dried completely, cover with strips of silver foil. Push the covered hook into the neck of the bottle.

Cutlass

Use a tightly-fitting leather belt to keep your cutlass to hand.

! 6 Trace off the template on pages 254-255 on to thick card and cut out. Paint the handle black and cover the blade with silver foil.

Team up a stripy T-shirt and a rolled up pair of jeans to create this pirate look.

North American Indian

Materials

thin card

fringe

ribbon

chunky wool

plastic tape

2 elastic bands

beads

feathers

pillowcase

Invite all your friends to a pow wow. They'll need to bring a pillowcase each!

Dress

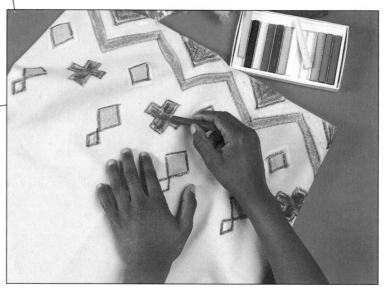

1 Make slits for your head and arms in the pillowcase. Decorate the front of the dress with fabric crayons.

2 Sew fringe around the arm holes and along the hem of the skirt. Thread beads on to the feathers and sew on to the dress.

Headband

3 Cut a strip of card long enough to go around your head with an overlap. Decorate the front with a strip of plastic tape. Tape a feather to the back.

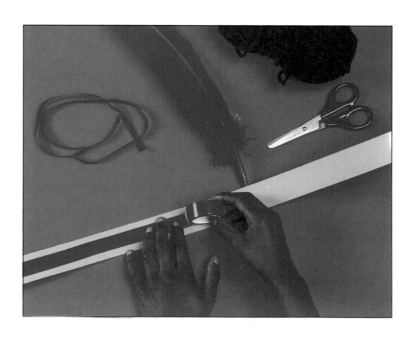

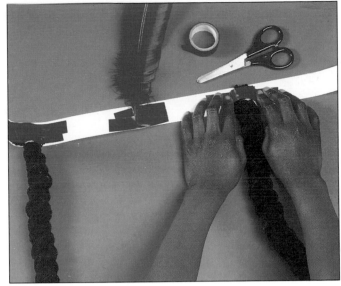

4 Cut the wool into lengths. Divide into 2 bunches. Wrap an elastic band around the top of each bunch. Plait the wool bunches. Securely tie ribbon around the bottom of each plait.

5 Tape the plaits to the inside of the headband, one on either side. Fit the finished headband around your head and staple the ends together.

To become an Indian chief, add more feathers to the headband and throw a patterned blanket across your back.

To make a papoose, follow the instructions on page 228 to make a cone from card. Decorate with fringe. Keep on your back with a long piece of cord threaded through the cone.

225

Cowboy

Before riding off into the sunset, you'll need a pair of spurs for your boots and a horse, of course!

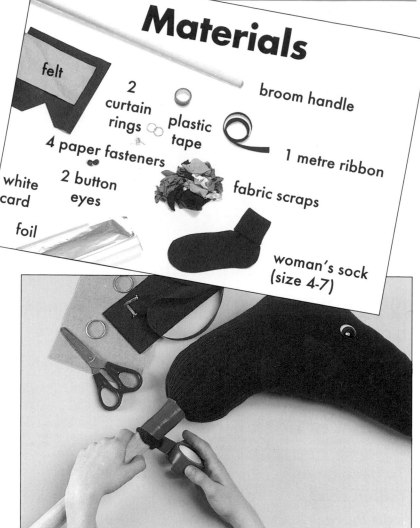

Materials

felt, 2 curtain rings, plastic tape, broom handle, 4 paper fasteners, 1 metre ribbon, white card, 2 button eyes, fabric scraps, foil, woman's sock (size 4-7)

Horse

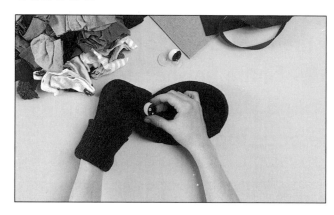

1 Push the eyes through the toe of the sock and secure on the inside with the studs. Stuff the sock with fabric scraps.

2 Push the broom handle into the sock and wind the tape securely around it.

3 Cut a fringe along one side of a strip of felt and glue to the top of the horse's head. Cut out 2 large triangular felt ears, fold in half and sew on.

4 Thread the rings on to ribbon long enough to go around the horse's nose with a 2 cm overlap. Glue the ribbon ends together and leave to dry. Thread the remaining ribbon on to the rings and fix with paper fasteners.

Spurs

5 Cut 2 stars (template page 255) and 4 strips measuring 10 x 2 cm from the card. Cover with foil.

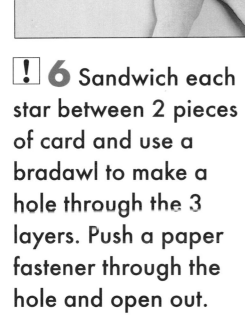

To complete the look, wear a cowboy hat, checked shirt, scarf and jeans; make a sheriff's badge using the template on page 255.

! **6** Sandwich each star between 2 pieces of card and use a bradawl to make a hole through the 3 layers. Push a paper fastener through the hole and open out.

To fix the spurs to your boots, stick a piece of double-sided tape to the inside of the pieces of card. Remove the backing and press firmly on to the back of each boot.

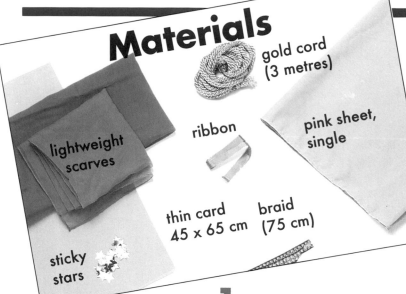

Materials

gold cord (3 metres)

lightweight scarves

ribbon

pink sheet, single

thin card 45 x 65 cm

braid (75 cm)

sticky stars

Princess

A fairytale princess costume that can be adapted easily into a wise wizard outfit.

Cone hat

1 Fold the card in half along its longest edge. Mark on a triangle and cut out. You now have 2 card triangles the same size.

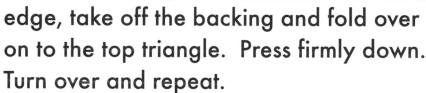

2 Lay one triangle on top of the other, so that 1.5 cm of the bottom triangle can be seen. Put double-sided tape along this edge, take off the backing and fold over on to the top triangle. Press firmly down. Turn over and repeat.

3 Trim the brim into a circle by cutting off the pointed ends. Decorate the cone with sticky stars all over and glue braid around the brim.

4 Snip off the top of the cone. Push the scarves into the hole and tape to the inside.

Robe

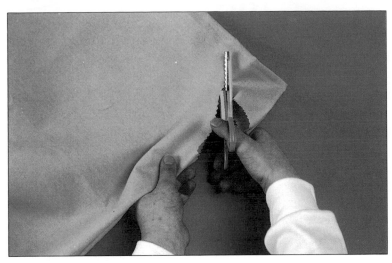

⚠ 5 Fold the sheet in half widthways, then in half again lengthways. To make an opening for your head, make a small triangular cut across the folded corner of the sheet with pinking shears.

Tape ribbon to the inside to tie on the hat.

Make a cloak from an old curtain. Thread with cord. Wrap around your shoulders and tie the cord under your chin.

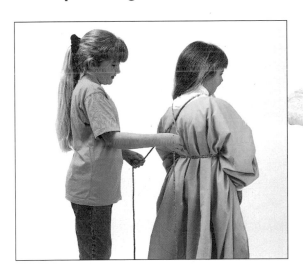

Adapt the look to become a wise wizard (star and moon templates on page 255).

⚠ 6 Slip the sheet over your head. Wrap the cord around your waist, cross over your chest, and take over your shoulders. Cross the cord over your back and bring around to the front of your waist. Tie in a knot.

Knight

A few trusty snips of the scissors and some bold bits of gluing will turn you into a brave knight.

pillowcase
Materials
red felt
1 cm wide elastic
silver foil
5 paper fasteners
silver card
2 silver-sprayed dishcloths
thick card

Tunic

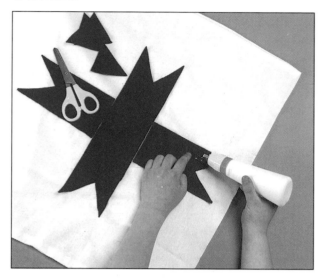

1 Make slits in the pillowcase for your arms and head. Cut 4 strips from the red felt. Snip a triangle into the end of each strip and stick on to the front of the tunic to make a cross.

Shield

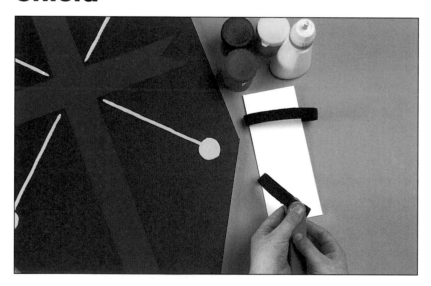

2 Draw a shield on to the card and cut out. Paint the front of the shield and leave to dry. Cut 2 pieces of elastic to fit around your forearm and staple into hoops.

3 Thread the hoops on to the card strip and glue on to the back of the shield.

230

Helmet

4 Staple a silver dishcloth to the centre of a silver card band, measuring 60 x 5 cm. Fit the band around your head and staple the ends together.

5 Fix a 30 x 4 cm strip of silver card from one side of the headband to the other using paper fasteners. Now fix a strip measuring 50 x 4 cm from the back to the front of the headband, leaving a bit of card hanging down at the front.

Slip the tunic over an outfit of grey sweatshirt, jogging bottoms, and wellington boots covered with silver foil. Wear a pair of grey woollen gloves.

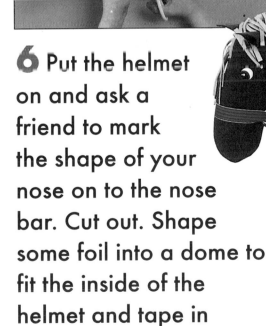

6 Put the helmet on and ask a friend to mark the shape of your nose on to the nose bar. Cut out. Shape some foil into a dome to fit the inside of the helmet and tape in place. Staple the second dishcloth in place.

To finish off the shield spray a large plastic pot lid with silver paint and glue to the centre.

Cut a 15-cm slit at the centre of the bottom edge of the front of the tunic.

231

Aladdin

If you've always wanted to be an Arabian prince or princess, you don't need a genie to make your wish come true. Just follow these simple instructions...

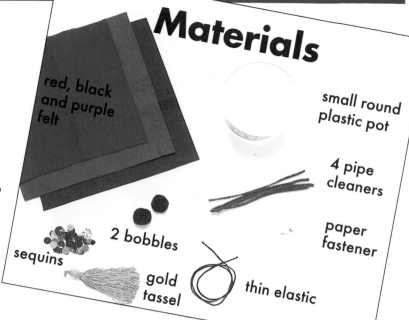

Materials

red, black and purple felt

small round plastic pot

4 pipe cleaners

paper fastener

2 bobbles

sequins

gold tassel

thin elastic

Fez

1 Draw around the base of the pot on to red felt and cut out. Fix the tassel to the felt circle with a paper fastener.

2 Cut a strip of red felt wide and long enough to go around the pot with a small overlap and glue in place. Trim the felt at the base to make it even.

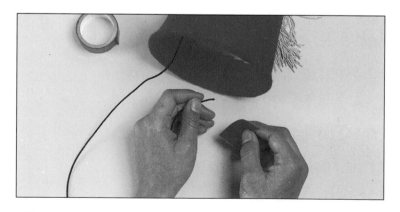

3 Cut slits along the felt at the top and base of the pot. Put glue on the felt tabs. Stick the glued tabs to the inside and base of the pot.

4 Glue the felt circle to the base of the pot. Tape a piece of elastic to either side of the pot on the inside.

232

Slippers

5 Cut 2 triangles from black felt and 2 from purple felt (template on page 254).

6 Glue 2 pipe cleaners along the long edges of a purple triangle. Glue a black triangle on top. Repeat with the other 2 triangles.

For Aladdin's trousers, take an old pair of silky adult pyjama bottoms and sew some elastic into the hem.

7 To decorate the slippers glue sequins on top of the black triangles. Sew a bobble to the tip. Bend the end of the slippers into a curl. Attach to a pair of plimsoles with double-sided tape.

To become an Arabian princess drape yourself in silky material.

Wrap a silk scarf around your waist and keep in place with a brooch.

233

Mad Robot

Recycle your rubbish and turn yourself into a mad robot.

Body

! **1** Cut the flaps from the box. Cut holes in the top and side of the box large enough for your head and arms to go through. Glue the packaging to the box.

Keep any gold or coloured foil packaging aside for later.

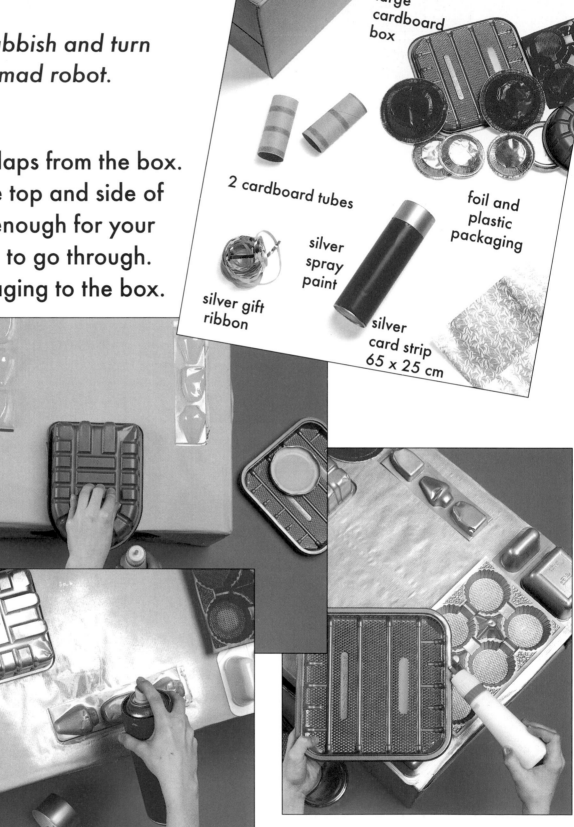

Materials

large cardboard box

2 cardboard tubes

silver gift ribbon

silver spray paint

foil and plastic packaging

silver card strip 65 x 25 cm

! **2** Spray the box and the 2 cardboard tubes with the silver spray paint.

3 Glue the gold and coloured foil packaging to the box.

4 Cut a letterbox slit in the centre of the card strip for you to see out of. Overlap the ends of the card strip to make a tube and staple together.

5 Cut a round hole on either side large enough to push the silver cardboard tubes into. Curl the silver ribbon using closed scissor blades and tape to the inside of the tube.

Wear the body over an outfit of grey jogging bottoms and grey sweatshirt. Cover a pair of wellington boots with silver foil.

Cut the top and bottom off of 2 plastic bottles. Spray with silver paint. Wear over a pair of plastic household gloves that have also been sprayed silver. Alternatively wear a pair of grey woollen gloves.

235

Hallowe'en

Three super scary looks that are so good you won't want to wait until Hallowe'en to try them out!

Witch's hat

Materials
red and black shredded tissue-paper

black net

thick red paper

2 large sheets of thick black paper

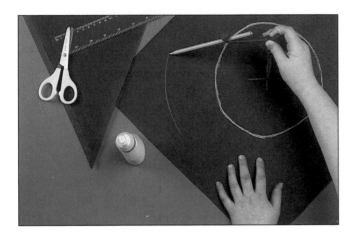

1 Make a cone from 1 sheet of paper (see page 228). Draw around the base of the cone on to the second sheet of paper. Draw on another circle 7 cm larger in diameter than the first.

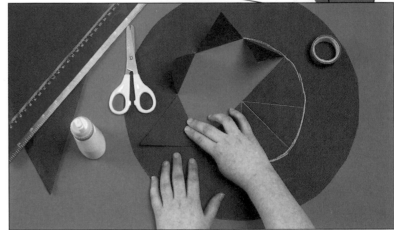

2 Use a ruler to divide the inner circle into 8 equal sections. Starting from the centre, cut along these lines and bend back the triangular tabs.

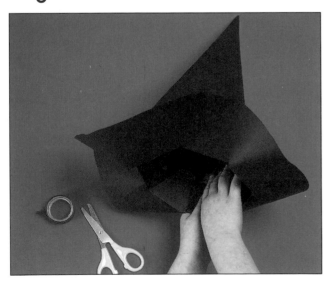

3 Put the cone over the brim. Tape the tabs to the inside.

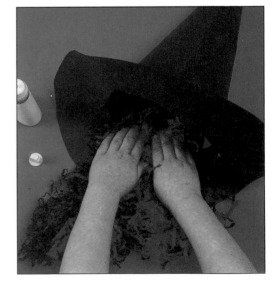

4 Glue shredded paper all around the brim of the hat, leaving a small opening for your face.

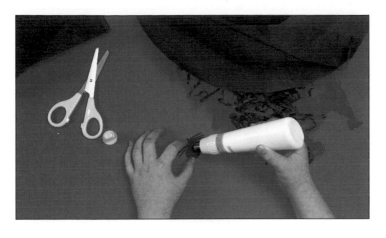

5 Tape a triangle of net from the top of the cone to the brim to make a spider's web. Glue red and black paper spiders (templates page 254) to the net.

Ghost

Cut 2 eye holes in an old sheet. For a really spooky effect, paint a ghoulish face on to the sheet with fabric paints.

Witch

Cut openings for your head and arms in a black bin liner. Cut star and moon shapes from gold and silver paper (templates page 255) and glue to the front of the bin liner.

Dracula

Wear a black sweatshirt over a white shirt and a pair of black jogging bottoms. For the cloak, cut a zig-zag pattern along one edge of a bin liner and pin it to the arms and back of the sweatshirt. Make a bow tie from a piece of white crêpe paper held at the centre with a hoop of white card stapled in place.

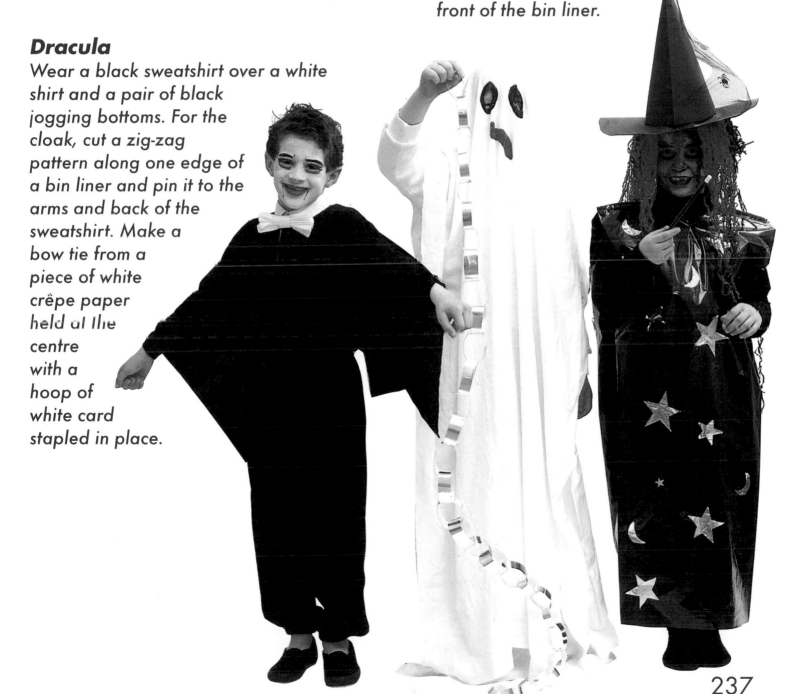

237

Christmas Present

Give your friends and family a surprise by wrapping yourself up for Christmas.

Materials

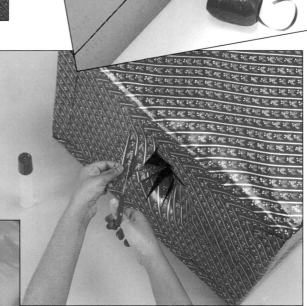

printed wrapping paper

metallic paper

large cardboard box

gift ribbon

Christmas card

! **1** Cut the flaps from the box. Cut holes for your arms and head. Cover with wrapping paper.

2 At the head and arm openings cut triangular tabs from the paper. Glue the tabs to the inside of the box.

3 For a decorative ribbon glue wide strips of metallic paper around the box.

4 Cut a large square of metallic paper. Fold over the edge of the paper by 2 cm and press down. Turn over and fold over by 2 cm again. Repeat until all the paper has been folded.

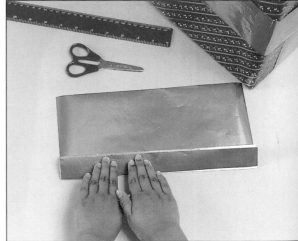

5 Fold in half and staple the top 2 edges together to make a fan. Put a length of double-sided tape along the bottom of the fan, remove the backing and press down firmly on to the box to the side of the head hole.

Tie the Christmas card gift tag around your wrist.

Wear the Christmas present over an outfit of leotard and tights or sweatshirt and jogging bottoms.

6 Punch a hole in the top left-hand corner of the Christmas card. Thread the ribbon through the hole.

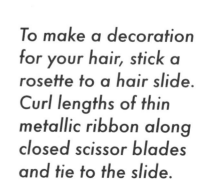

To make a decoration for your hair, stick a rosette to a hair slide. Curl lengths of thin metallic ribbon along closed scissor blades and tie to the slide.

239

Tooth Fairy

Turn an old net curtain into a wonderful pair of glittering fairy wings.

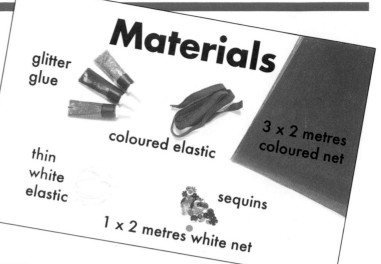

glitter glue

Materials

coloured elastic

thin white elastic

3 x 2 metres coloured net

sequins

1 x 2 metres white net

Wings

1 Use glitter glue to decorate the white net with swirling patterns. Hang up to dry.

2 Sew 2 lines of running stitches up the centre of the net, leaving long threads at either end. Gently pull the threads to gather the net and secure with a knot.

3 Make 2 loops from white elastic large enough to go around your wrists and sew to the top 2 corners of the wings.

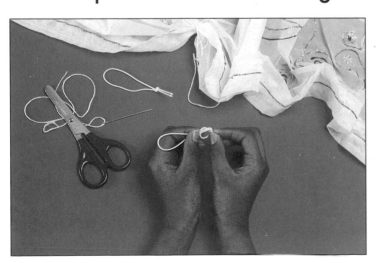

Skirt

4 Fold the coloured net in half. Punch holes along the folded edge.

5 Carefully thread the coloured elastic through the punched holes. Knot the ends of the elastic together to fit around your waist.

To transform yourself into a butterfly, make a pair of wings from a piece of old white sheet decorated with fabric paints. Twist 2 pipe cleaners around a hairband and curl the ends.

To make a tooth necklace thread polystyrene packing chips on to coloured cotton. Don't forget to take a bag to carry your tooth money in!

Make a wand from a garden stick stuck into a star cut out from corrugated cardboard (template page 255). Cover with silver foil.

6 Glue sequins all over the skirt and hang up to dry.

Wear your fairy wings and skirt over a brightly-coloured pair of tights and matching top. Use safety pins to pin the wings to the back of the top and slip the elastic hoops over your wrists.

Bumble Bee

Materials

black elastic

gold glitter pen

plastic-covered wire

black tights

black plastic tape

cotton wool

1 Bend 1 metre of wire into a hoop. Make another wire hoop. Join the hoops by twisting the ends together. Cover the twisted ends with cotton wool padding and keep in place with tape.

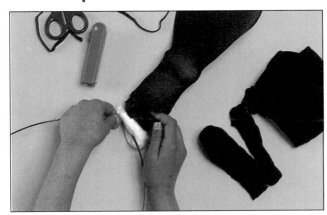

2 Cut the legs from the tights and stretch over the wire hoops. Overlap and tape together. Cut 2 40-cm pieces of black elastic and staple into hoops. Slip over the wings and tape to either side of the padded bar.

Thread a long pipe cleaner through the weave on top of a black balaclava. Sew a yellow bobble to each end.

Wear the bumble bee wings over an outfit of black leggings and a black sweatshirt that has had yellow ribbon strips double-sided across the front of it.

3 Reshape the wire hoops. Decorate by gluing lines of glitter over the front of the wings.

242

Templates

For instructions on how to trace a template turn to page 256.

Fish in a Net
(pages 16-17)
SMALL FISH

Fish in a Net
(pages 16-17)
LARGE FISH

Surprise Tree
(pages 18-19)
CAT

Balancing Butterfly
(pages 24-25)
BUTTERFLY

Surprise Tree
(pages 18-19)
BIRD

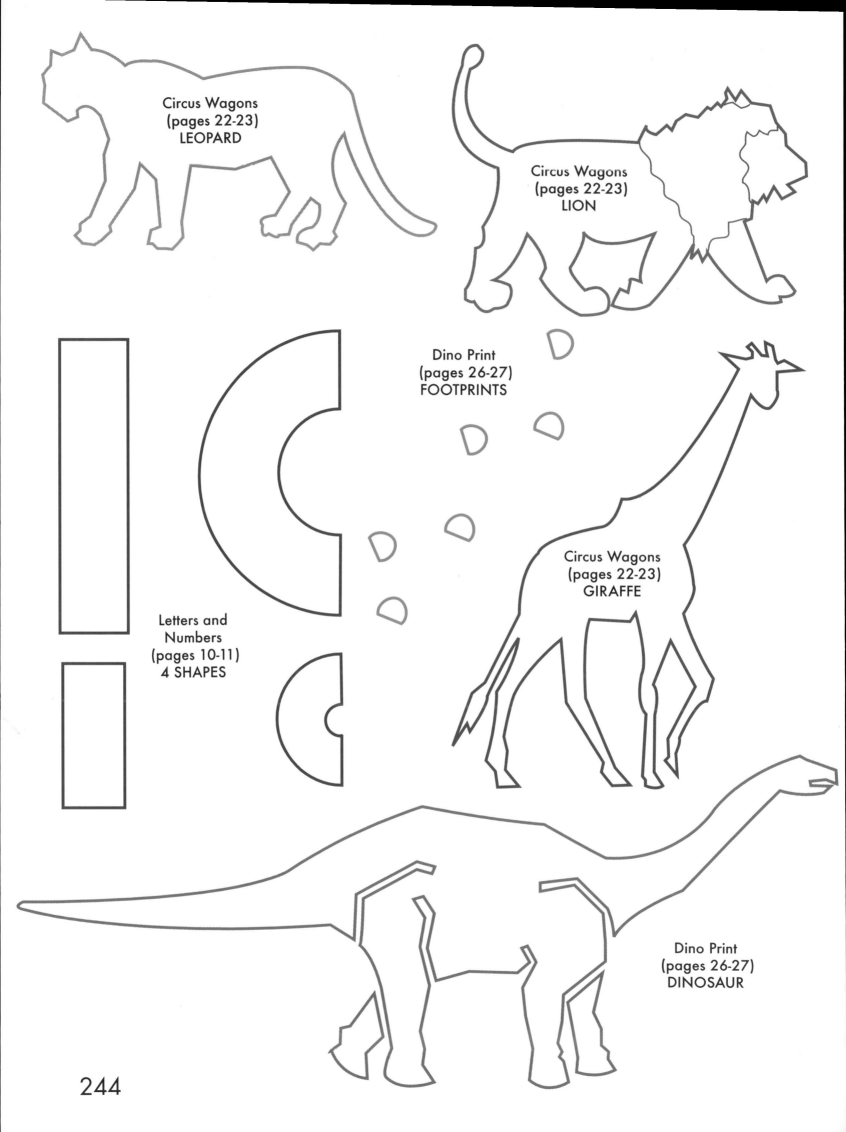

Circus Wagons
(pages 22-23)
LEOPARD

Circus Wagons
(pages 22-23)
LION

Dino Print
(pages 26-27)
FOOTPRINTS

Letters and
Numbers
(pages 10-11)
4 SHAPES

Circus Wagons
(pages 22-23)
GIRAFFE

Dino Print
(pages 26-27)
DINOSAUR

244

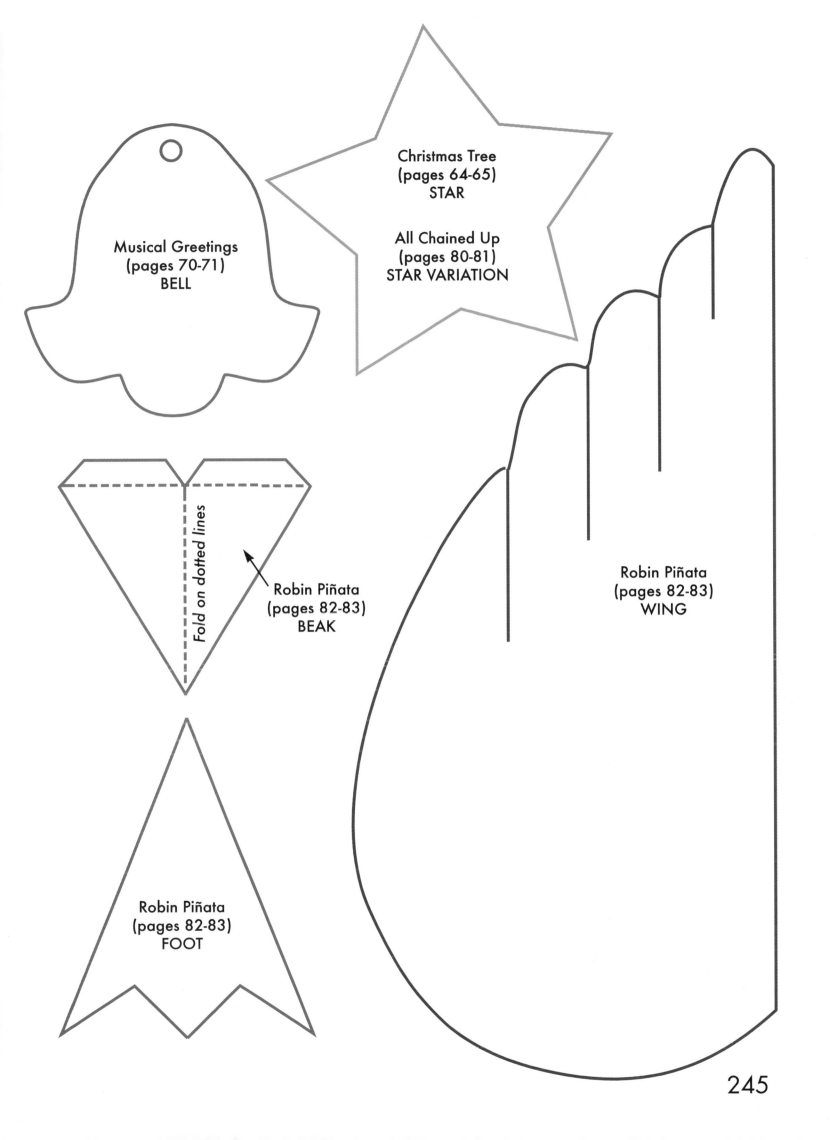

Musical Greetings
(pages 70-71)
BELL

Christmas Tree
(pages 64-65)
STAR

All Chained Up
(pages 80-81)
STAR VARIATION

Fold on dotted lines

Robin Piñata
(pages 82-83)
BEAK

Robin Piñata
(pages 82-83)
WING

Robin Piñata
(pages 82-83)
FOOT

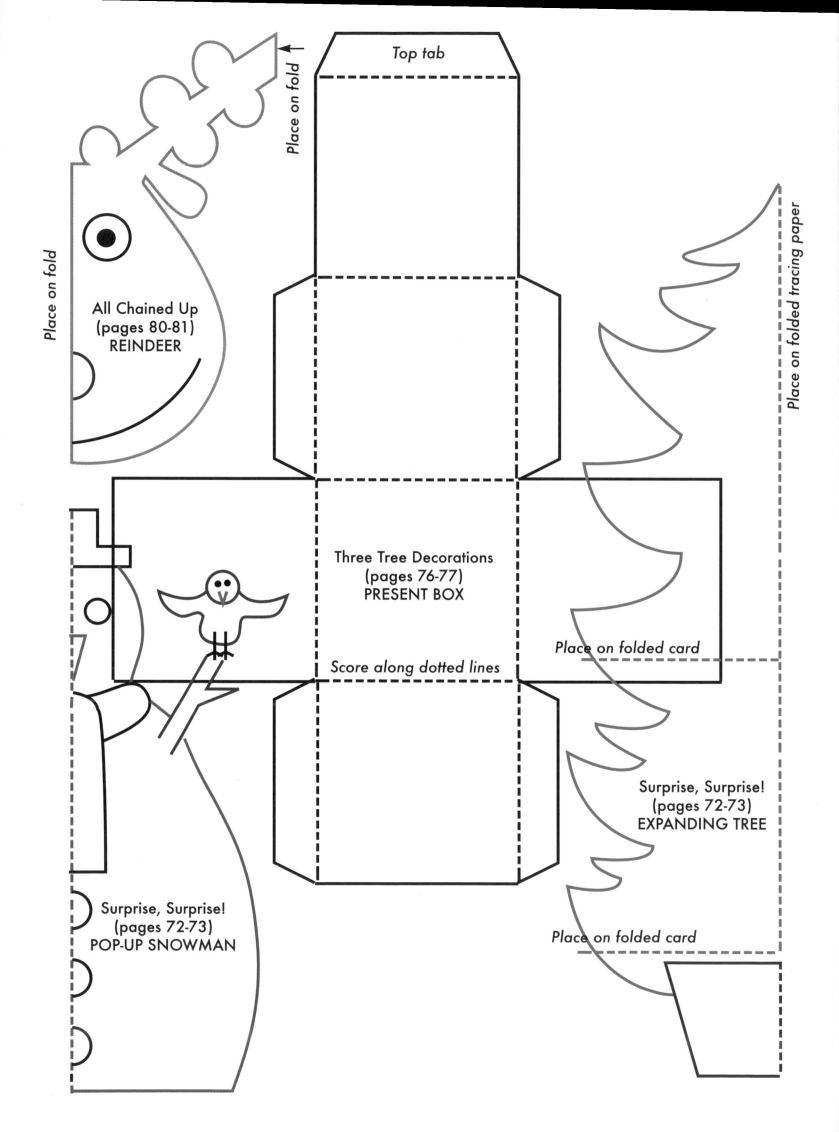

Place on fold

Top tab

Place on folded tracing paper

All Chained Up
(pages 80-81)
REINDEER

Place on fold

Three Tree Decorations
(pages 76-77)
PRESENT BOX

Place on folded card

Score along dotted lines

Surprise, Surprise!
(pages 72-73)
EXPANDING TREE

Surprise, Surprise!
(pages 72-73)
POP-UP SNOWMAN

Place on folded card

Shell Necklace
(alternative
pages 122-123)
SHELL

Badges For
Everyone
(pages 130-
131)
HEART

Shell Necklace
(alternative
pages 122-123)
SHELL

Badges For
Everyone
(pages 130-
131)
STAR

Snake
Charmers
(pages 126-
127)

Autumn Leaf
Necklace
(pages 122-
123)
LEAVES

247

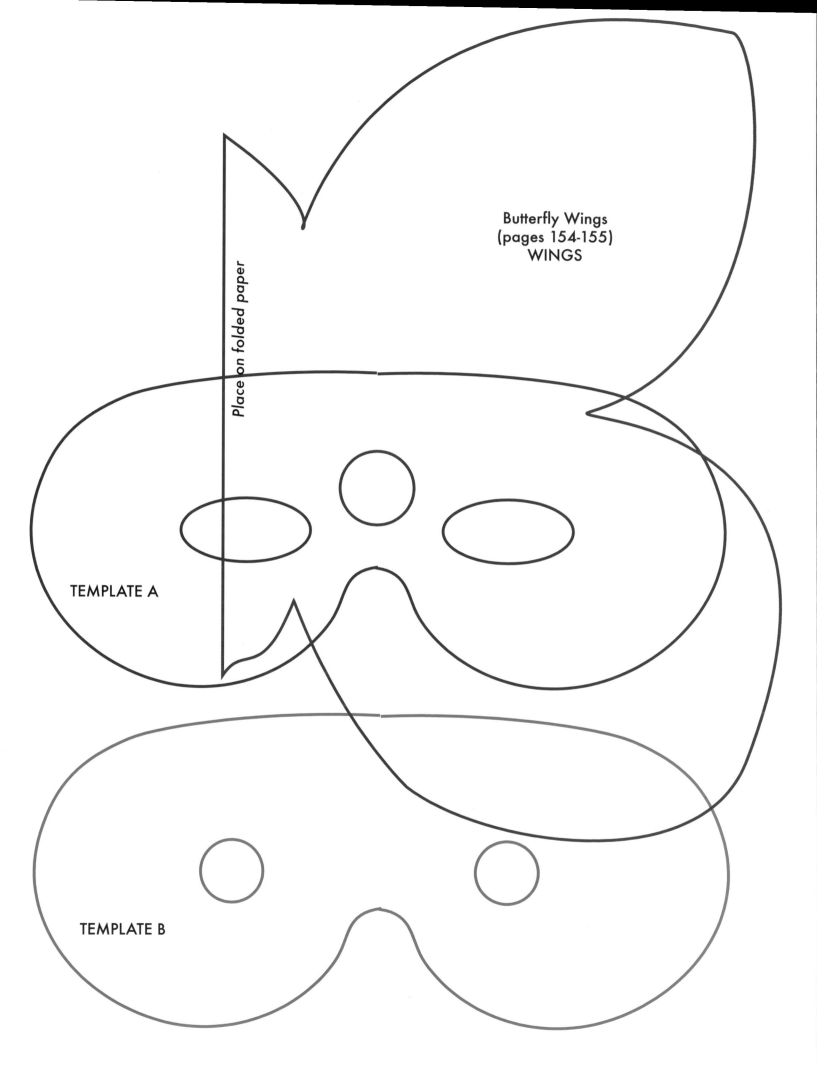

Butterfly Wings
(pages 154-155)
WINGS

Place on folded paper

TEMPLATE A

TEMPLATE B

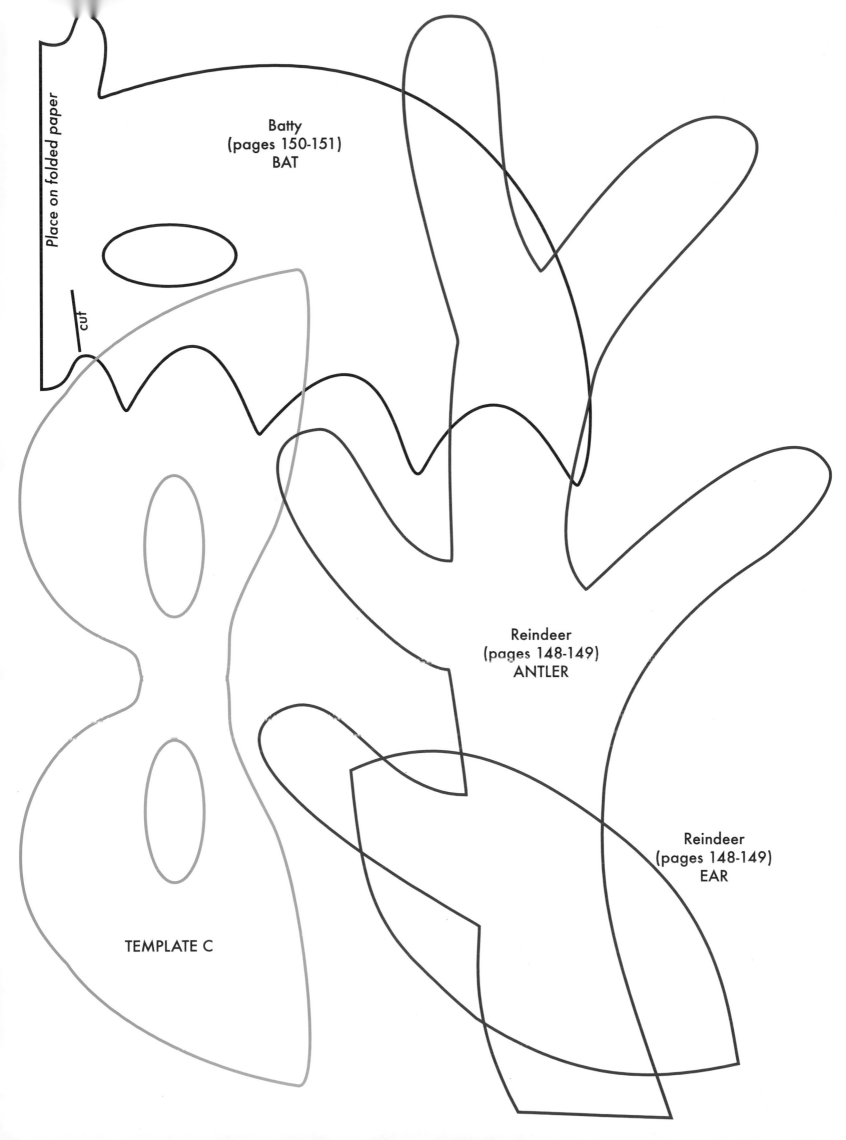

Place on folded paper

cut

Batty
(pages 150-151)
BAT

Reindeer
(pages 148-149)
ANTLER

Reindeer
(pages 148-149)
EAR

TEMPLATE C

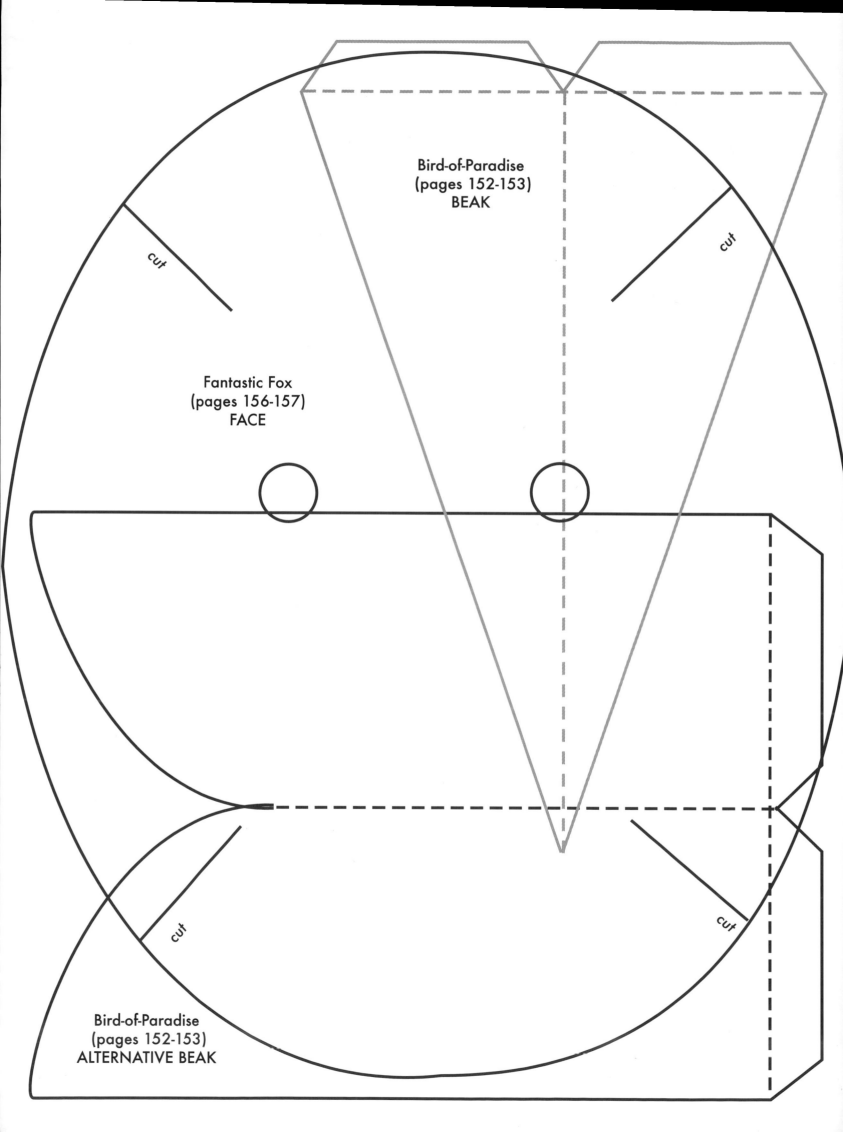

Bird-of-Paradise
(pages 152-153)
BEAK

Fantastic Fox
(pages 156-157)
FACE

cut

cut

cut

cut

Bird-of-Paradise
(pages 152-153)
ALTERNATIVE BEAK

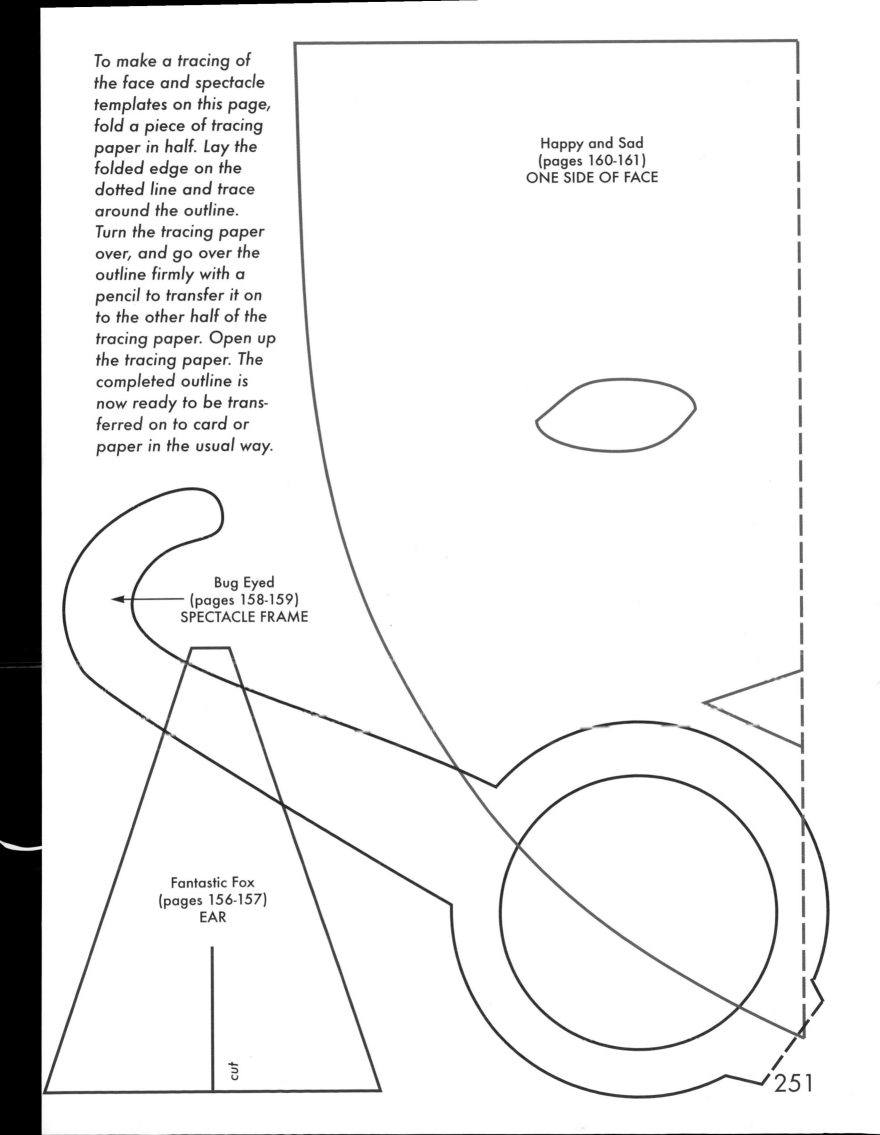

To make a tracing of the face and spectacle templates on this page, fold a piece of tracing paper in half. Lay the folded edge on the dotted line and trace around the outline. Turn the tracing paper over, and go over the outline firmly with a pencil to transfer it on to the other half of the tracing paper. Open up the tracing paper. The completed outline is now ready to be transferred on to card or paper in the usual way.

Happy and Sad
(pages 160-161)
ONE SIDE OF FACE

Bug Eyed
(pages 158-159)
SPECTACLE FRAME

Fantastic Fox
(pages 156-157)
EAR

cut

251

Teddy Bear Pencil Holder
(pages 194-195)
HEAD

Cat Pencil Holder
(alternative pages
194-195)
HEAD

Mini Felt
Stockings
(pages 216-217)
SNOWMAN'S
HAT

Buttefly Card
(pages 196-197)
BUTTERFLY

Mini Felt Stockings
(pages 216-217)
SNOWMAN

252

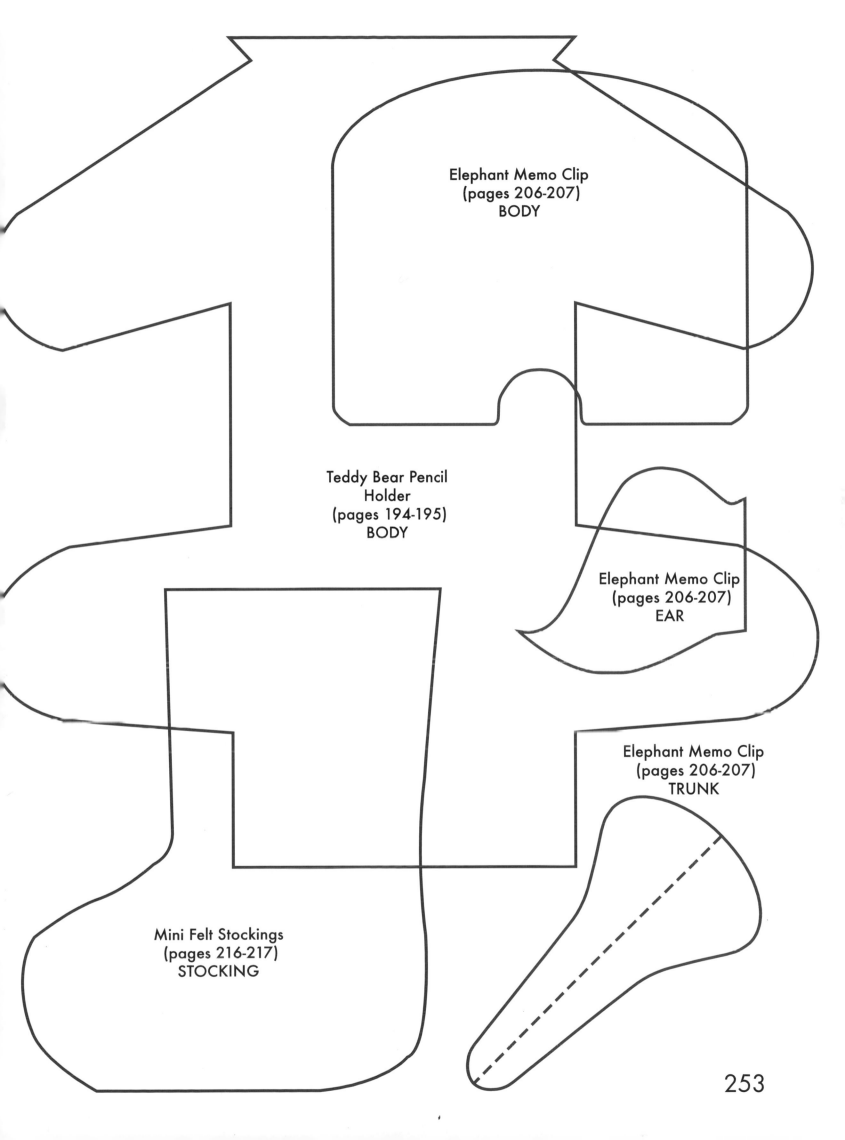

Elephant Memo Clip
(pages 206-207)
BODY

Teddy Bear Pencil
Holder
(pages 194-195)
BODY

Elephant Memo Clip
(pages 206-207)
EAR

Elephant Memo Clip
(pages 206-207)
TRUNK

Mini Felt Stockings
(pages 216-217)
STOCKING

253

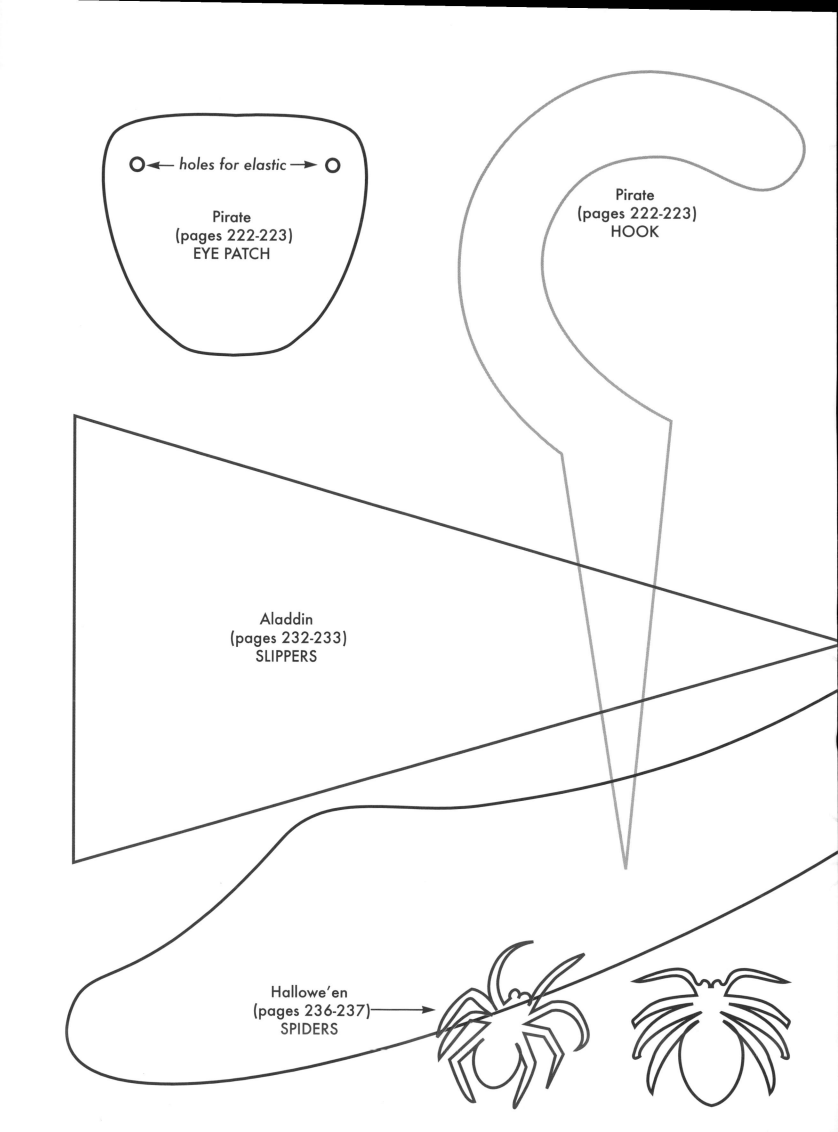

← holes for elastic →

Pirate
(pages 222-223)
EYE PATCH

Pirate
(pages 222-223)
HOOK

Aladdin
(pages 232-233)
SLIPPERS

Hallowe'en
(pages 236-237)
SPIDERS

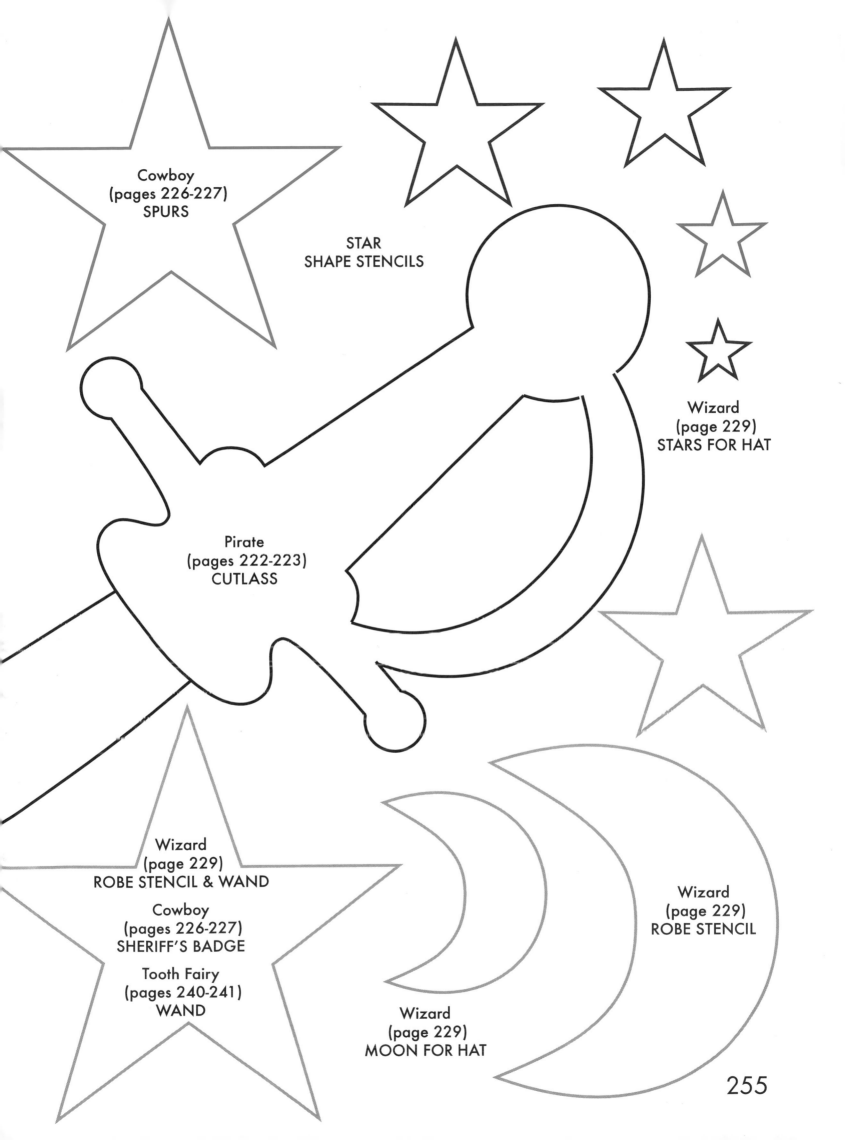

Cowboy
(pages 226-227)
SPURS

STAR
SHAPE STENCILS

Wizard
(page 229)
STARS FOR HAT

Pirate
(pages 222-223)
CUTLASS

Wizard
(page 229)
ROBE STENCIL & WAND

Cowboy
(pages 226-227)
SHERIFF'S BADGE

Tooth Fairy
(pages 240-241)
WAND

Wizard
(page 229)
ROBE STENCIL

Wizard
(page 229)
MOON FOR HAT

255

Advice to parents

The information on the following pages should enable you to help your child to get the most from this book.

WHAT YOU NEED TO PROVIDE
All that is required is an area where your child can work undisturbed, a few basic tools and readily-available materials, and your encouragement.

MAKING SPACE
A table surface is not always the best place for making things; it can be very frustrating for the child to be told to clear away for dinner just as she is in the middle of something. The best solution is to lay an old sheet down on the floor in a corner of the room where the child will not be in anybody's way.

CLEARING UP
You can minimize the mess by making sure that the work space is well covered and by covering up your child before she begins work. Buy a wipe-clean plastic apron, or make a smock out of an old shirt. Encourage your child to help you clean up afterwards. Wash out paint pots and brushes so that they are ready for use next time. Store the dry brushes bristle end up in a pot or jar. Clean the nozzle of the glue bottle to prevent it blocking up.

MATERIALS AND TOOLS
It is important that all tools and materials provided for craft activities are simple and safe to use.

Paint: Always have the basic set of colours in stock: red, blue, yellow, black and white. All other colours can be mixed from these. Encourage your child to explore colour mixing for herself and provide her with an old plate to mix paint on. Buy ready-mixed water-based paint in the economy size. These last for ages and they mix well. Always make sure that paint has dried before going on to the next step in the project.

Felt-tip pens: A good set of felt-tip pens is ideal for decoration when the child either has no time, or is not willing, to wait for paint to dry (particularly suitable for the younger child). Felt-tip pens are available that will wash out of clothes easily.

Paper and card: Always keep both white and coloured paper and card in the house. Paper and card can be expensive to buy, so do make a point of trying to recycle materials wherever possible. Save cereal packets, old cardboard boxes, newspapers, clothes packaging and wallpaper off-cuts.

Glue: Solvent-free PVA adhesive is recommended as it is versatile, clean, strong and safe.

Scissors: For the sake of safety children should use small scissors with round-ended metal blades and plastic handles. Although these are fine for cutting paper and thin card, they will not cut thick card and this is best done by you. This will often require a craft knife.

Varnish: A light coat of varnish will give finished items a shiny finish and help them to last longer. You should buy non-toxic varnish that is suitable for children to use, available from most art and craft shops. Always ensure that the varnish has completely dried before adding any decorations.

MODELLING
Play dough is simple to make, but as it needs cooking, adult assistance is required. Play dough can be stored in an airtight container in the refrigerator; when it is taken from the refrigerator it may require a few drops of oil to be kneaded into it to make it pliable.

Salt dough can be baked in an oven, decorated and varnished, so that models made with it can be kept forever. Salt dough is best made the day before it is required. Store in a plastic bag in the refrigerator. Before using, knead well on a lightly-floured board. Before baking modelled articles, brush lightly with a little water to give a good finish. Place items on a lightly-greased baking tray or on baking parchment. Salt dough should be cooked in the oven on a low heat (120°C/350°F/gas ½). Small articles will take 1–2 hours, large models will need 3–4 hours. Better still, cook overnight on the lowest setting. If possible turn the salt dough models over halfway through baking to ensure that they are cooked through.

NOTE: Salt dough cannot be cooked in a microwave oven.

Air-hardening clay does not need a kiln to harden it; it will dry hard in a few days if left in a cool, dry place. It can be bought in 500 g or 1 kg packets from art and craft shops. Once opened, the clay will keep if wrapped in foil or cling film and placed in a plastic bag.

Papier Mâché is a cheap and versatile modelling material made from old newspapers and a flour and water paste. There are two methods for making papier mâché:

The Layered Method: Lay strips of torn newspaper over a mould and paste each layer with a flour paste made from approximately 2 heaped tablespoons plain flour mixed with 100 ml water.

The Pulp Method: Tear newspaper into small squares and mix with a flour paste made from approximately 2 heaped tablespoons plain flour to 200 ml water to make a malleable pulp.

Before decorating, papier mâché models must be left for several days to dry out completely in a dry, warm place, such as an airing cupboard, otherwise fungus will form.

Modelling plaster (plaster of Paris) can be purchased from most art and craft shops. It is normally mixed at 2 portions of plaster to 1 of water, but this may vary slightly. Plastic packaging from food products make excellent moulds. Wipe the mould with neat washing-up liquid so that it will release the plaster cast easily once it has set. If the mould will not come away, it can be cut with scissors and carefully stripped.

MAKING A TEMPLATE
To make a reusable card template, lay a piece of tracing paper over the required template on pages 243–255. Draw around the outline with a pencil. Turn the tracing paper over and scribble over the pencil outline. Turn the tracing paper over again and lay down onto a piece of thick card. Draw around the pencil outline. Remove the tracing paper. The outline of the traced shape on the card may be quite faint. Go over it with black felt-tip pen. Cut out and label the card template and keep it in a safe place. Use the card template to draw around as many times as is needed onto paper, card or fabric.